POWDERED PEAS
AND
OTHER BLESSINGS

POWDERED PEAS
AND
OTHER BLESSINGS

*Life in An Orphanage in
Naples, Italy*

Christine Foster Meloni

To order additional copies of this book, contact:
Xlibris Corporation
1-888-795-4274
www.Xlibris.com
Orders@Xlibris.com
17371

CONTENTS

In loving memory of
Anne Acoca
Massimo Finoia
Franco Maccarrone

ACKNOWLEDGMENTS

What an extraordinary delight it was for me to speak with the 21 former residents of Casa Materna whose stories you will read in this book. I talked with most of them in person during my visits to Italy in 1993 and 1995. The others I communicated with through letters. They were all eager to answer my questions and to share their personal stories with me. I would like to thank them all from the bottom of my heart for their enthusiasm and their kindness.

I would also like to thank many others who assisted in the preparation of this book.

My friend Dr. Dona De Sanctis inspired me to write this book. She assisted in the preparation of the questionnaires and wrote the historical sketches. As editor-in-chief of Ambassador *magazine, she published the narrative of Franco Maccarrone and the readers' response to this piece was overwhelmingly positive.*

My husband Andrea Meloni continuously encouraged and supported me throughout the project. He believed in its importance and assisted in many ways. My children Adriano, Marcello, and Nicoletta were as usual among my most ardent cheerleaders.

My friends Anne Acoca, Robin Alexander, George Bozzini, Nancy Burwell Dicken, Mary Niebuhr, Kirky Munson Otto, and Kay Wright carefully read drafts of this book and made valuable comments.

Dr. Dennis Brunn, former president and current member of the Executive Board of the U.S. Casa Materna Society, provided useful advice and moral support.

The Rev. Fred Dole, another former president and current member of the U.S. Casa Materna Society, contributed his talents as professional photographer. He takes credit for most of the recent photos.

I am especially indebted to Rosaria Russo Vincenzi, a former resident of Casa Materna who served several years as its dedicated director, for her tireless efforts on behalf of this book, for her enthusiasm, and for her faithful support. Without her nothing could have been accomplished. She will have my enduring gratitude and affection.

PREFACE

A COLLEGE STUDENT'S DREAM SUMMER

By Christine Meloni

How lucky I was! I had managed to land a summer job at a Home for children in Naples. I was a 21-year old college student majoring in Italian and passionately in love with Italy. I set sail aboard the USS Aurelia in June as soon as I finished my final exams of the year.

It was the summer of 1962. My relationship with Casa Materna, therefore, goes back many years. That summer I taught English to the children in the mornings and translated correspondence in the office in the afternoons. I remember the lovely Bay of Naples, the stunning blue sky, the tall, proud palm trees, and the fragrant lemons but most of all I have fond memories of the people.

I will always cherish my memories of Pastor Emanuele Santi, Director of the Home. He could have become a concert violinist but he chose to become a Methodist pastor. He continued to love music and to share this love with others. He hired a band director and organized a boys' band. He personally attended the practices every evening, and he always invited me to join him. He conducted all of the religious services—every morning before school, every evening before dinner, and on Sundays. He was kind to the volunteers and frequently took us out in the evenings for ice cream (probably the very best ice cream in the world can be found in Naples).

Dr. Teofilo Santi was very busy outside of Casa Materna in his role as doctor so I saw him much less often than I saw his brother Pastor Emanuele. It was a joyous occasion for all of us when he was present. He always made it a point to greet each one of the many children personally. (There were about 350 children in residence at the time.) His wife Signora Livia was an impressive woman. I marveled at the way she was able to maintain discipline and order with such a large number of children.

And, of course, the children. They were so much fun to be with! They were warm and affectionate and full of spunk. Their joie de vivre was contagious. Being an American, I was somewhat of a novelty to them. They sought me out constantly. They wanted me to play with them, to talk with them. They laughed at my Italian. They asked me tons of questions. They told me lots of stories. They introduced me to their families on visiting days. They slipped me secret notes. They made me laugh and they sometimes made me cry. Each one was special.

I have kept in touch with Casa Materna over the years because I am so impressed with the wonderful work that this institution is doing for the disadvantaged children of Naples and of southern Italy as well as immigrant children from other countries such as Somalia and Ethiopia.

As I listened to former residents talk about growing up at Casa Materna, I was moved. I heard many stories. What struck me the most forcefully was the sense of deep gratitude they all felt for their experience at Casa Materna. What was so special about Casa Materna? Why did these adults who grew up away from their families have such fond memories of growing up in a children's home? You will find some of the answers in the personal narratives of the 21 individuals I selected from different periods of Casa Materna's history as representative.

Springfield, Virginia
November 2002

Note: The interviews were conducted in Italian, audiotaped, and transcribed. The transcripts were then translated into English for the purposes of this book. An Italian edition will be forthcoming.

Anna, Casa Materna employee (left) and Christine (right)
Casa Materna, summer 1962
Photo: Christine Meloni

CHAPTER 1

INVITATION TO A BIRTHDAY PARTY

"Want to buy some matches, Signore?"

The sun was shining brightly on that warm June afternoon in 1905. Pastor Santi was taking a stroll through his Neapolitan neighborhood while his wife Ersilia prepared his special birthday dinner.

Papà Riccardo Santi turned his head to see who had called out to him. He looked down and saw two wide-eyed children staring up at him imploringly. He was struck by their sad appearance.

He asked them some questions. He found out that their names were Angelo and Rosetta and that they were four and three years old, respectively. Their mother worked as a maid, and they had never known their father. They were homeless and lived under a bridge. Impulsively, Pastor Santi decided to invite them to his birthday dinner. The children led him to their mother who readily gave her permission.

During this meal Papà and Mamma Santi made a decision that would change their lives and those of thousands of others. The Santis felt called to do something for these homeless children and asked their mother if they could raise them. She gratefully agreed. The Santis continued to take disadvantaged children into their home in Via dei Cimbri in Naples and thus Casa Materna was born. In 1920 the Methodist Church purchased the lovely summer villa of the Prince of Monaco on the Bay of Naples in Portici where Casa Materna has been located to this day.

Papà and Mamma Santi had four children of their own, Emanuele, Luisa, Teofilo, and Fabio. Emanuele moved to the United

States at a young age and became the pastor of a church in Tuckahoe, New York. He was a wonderful ambassador for Casa Materna and set up a vast network of supporters in the U.S. Luisa married an American and moved to the United States as well. She and her husband had five children.

Teofilo became a doctor and remained in the Naples area, serving the children of Casa Materna and the economically disadvantaged of the area. Fabio became a lawyer and served a term as mayor of Portici. He succeeded his father as director of the Home. Fabio died tragically in a car accident. Upon his death Emanuele returned to Italy and took over as director. He remained director until his death in 1987. Coincidentally, Luisa and Teofilo also died in that same year.

Emanuele and Fabio never married. Teofilo married Signora Livia who immediately involved herself in the work of the home. Their daughter Daniela grew up surrounded by the other children. Eventually she became an elementary school teacher at Casa Materna. She married Luigi Capuano who served as co-director of the Home with Signora Livia, his mother-in-law. Daniela and Luigi have one son Cristiano who has chosen medicine as his profession, thus following in the steps of his grandfather Teofilo.

The important work begun in 1905 by Papà and Mamma Santi with Angelo and Rosetta continues today.

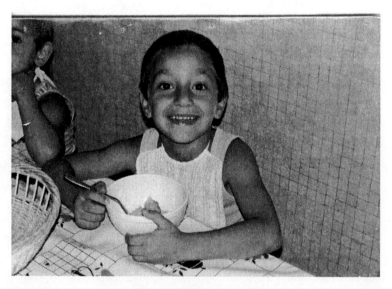

Enrico enjoying his dinner
Casa Materna, circa 1994
Photo: Casa Materna Archives

CHAPTER 2

THE EARLY YEARS: 1905-1920

Great Expectations and The Great War

Italy entered the 20th century with high hopes. Unified since 1870, Italians saw their industries, foreign trade, employment, and salaries grow rapidly. Despite the prosperity, thousands of southern Italians became part of the Great Migration to America that began in 1880. In 1913 alone, 870,000 of Italy's 35 million people left home—many of them forever. But even the Great Migration helped Italy prosper as successful immigrants sent millions of dollars home to less fortunate relatives.

The new century also saw the rise of imperialism and socialism in Italy. Proponents of imperialism, popularly known as "the new nationalism," wanted Italy to become a strong military power with a great empire. They believed that, as a great and powerful kingdom with a vast colonial empire, Italy would be both feared and respected. Meanwhile, Italy's workers and intellectuals began to favor the socialist principles of Karl Marx and their promise of significant social reform.

Swayed by these imperialistic and socialist tendencies, Italy launched its colonial wars in Libya in 1911. The next year, a young socialist became editor of his party's newspaper *Avanti!* His name— Benito Mussolini. A few years later he would rise to national and international fame.

In 1914, World War I broke out. Italy stayed neutral for a year and then entered the war against Austria and Germany, allied with France, Great Britain and Russia, whose leaders signed a secret treaty promising to give Italy territory that would secure its northern borders and its colonies in Africa.

Militarily and economically unprepared for war, Italy held its own for a while and then suffered a terrible defeat at the battle of Caporetto in the Italian Alps. The Italian troops recouped and fought valiantly in successive battles.

In 1918, the war ended but the victory was a hollow one for Italy. For the war, Italy had mobilized 5.2 million men, nearly 15 percent of its population. In the three and a half years of fighting, 680,000 Italian soldiers were killed and another 947,000 wounded. Despite its participation and contributions to the war effort, Italy was not treated fairly by its allies. Although its own strategic boundaries were greatly increased, Italy did not get the colonies promised by its allies. England added 2.5 million square miles to its empire and France, 1 million. Italy got 100,000 square miles, most of them African desert.

Italy believed that its allies had taken care of their own interests and that there was little to be expected from them in the future . . . unless Italy was strong enough militarily to act independently. This disillusionment set the scene for the next two decades, the most disastrous in modern Italian history.

In 1919, Benito Mussolini founded the Fascist party in Milan with 150 young men, most of them embittered veterans of "The Great War." The Party's main tenets were the unquestioned supremacy of the State, the banning of all political opposition, and the winning of an Italian "empire."

During these years Papà and Mamma Santi were living in Via dei Cimbri, a street near the port of Naples, and began to take poor children into their home in 1905.

Gilda De Turris was one of the first children to benefit from the Santis' love. She lived at Casa Materna for seven years, from 1910 to 1917. Her son Massimo, who became a respected and influential professor of economics at the University of Rome, says that Casa Materna exerted a strong influence on her character and her way of thinking. She tried to transmit to her children the education and the values that she received there. She always shared her childhood experiences with great joy. Here Massimo recounts his mother's story.

Gilda's Straw Hat, Come Out!

Gilda's Story
(as told by her son Massimo Finoia)

My mother's mother, Assunta Giuliani, was on the verge of becoming a nun. At an early age she had entered a convent at the foot of Mount Vesuvius. When she reached the age of 21, the time came for her to take the vows of chastity, poverty, and obedience. However, before she took these vows, her Mother Superior sent her out of the convent, as was the custom, to say good-bye to the world that she was about to renounce.

While visiting some relatives, she met a young military man, Alfredo De Turris, a member of the Protestant community of Naples. He was surprised at seeing this young woman ready to renounce marriage and children, perhaps because he immediately admired her beauty, perhaps because the idea of a convent and of a life of renunciation was alien to his Protestant way of thinking. In any case he asked her if she was really aware of what she was giving up, if she really knew the world.

The two immediately fell in love and shortly thereafter, they were married. They had five children. But Alfredo died suddenly and left his wife a widow at the age of 30. She was unable to care for the five children on her own. The Protestant community came to her assistance and Casa Materna welcomed the two youngest daughters, Maria who was eight and Elvira who was six. The Santis decided to call my mother by her middle name Gilda in order to avoid confusion with two other girls with the name Maria.

One of my mother's fondest memories of Casa Materna was her participation in an historical play designed to inspire patriotism for the war effort. Her account of the play is the story that excited me the most and that I remember most vividly.

This play was performed during World War I. At the time the memory of the events leading to the unification of Italy in 1860 was very much alive, and the need for unity among Italians in wartime was very much recognized. Therefore, the play, which reconstructed the events of the unification of Italy, was very appropriate. The principal characters were Italy and the three capitals, Turin, Florence, and Rome. My mother represented Florence, Italy's second capital. She appeared on stage dressed in white with a sash with the colors of the Italian flag, and she received from Italy the task of being the capital until Rome was liberated. My mother had a sense of humor, and she used to tell us that she had been chosen for this role because her nose was like that of the Florentine Dante!

At Casa Materna the theater was not only an occasion for entertainment but also a means for the cultural and civic formation of the children, an opportunity for the children to learn the history of Italy and to learn to love it.

Another favorite story that she told us over and over again was the time she lost her hat. One day the children of Casa Materna went for a walk in a park. When it was time to go home, my mother discovered that her hat was missing. Everyone immediately began to look for it, running around and shouting, "Gilda's straw hat, come out!" And it **did** come out! This expression became a familiar one within our family. Whenever something was lost that we were sure would never be found, my mother encouraged us to look, saying, "Gilda's straw hat, come out!"

The Santis and the children at Casa Materna did not live in the midst of plenty. As a matter of fact, the deprivations were such that sometimes it was difficult to foresee what would be on the table the next day. In spite of this, the Santis were always serene and faithful. My mother often talked of Papà Santi's faith in God and how this faith was often rewarded.

Even if there was little to eat at times, the community always sat down at a carefully set table, and this gave everyone the feeling that the reality was not so desperate. My mother learned this lesson well. During the last months of World War II, food was scarce at our home, there was no bread, and, because of the bombing, we spent many hours in an air-raid shelter. However, I do not remember a single day in which my family did not sit down at a set table, even if only to eat boiled potatoes.

My mother left Casa Materna in 1917 at the age of 15 and went to work as a cashier at Gutteridge's, one of the largest Neapolitan shops at that time. The owners were English and, since they were Protestants, she probably obtained this position through Casa Materna.

In 1930 she married my father Vincenzo Finoia who had also lost his father at a very early age (at the age of 2). She left her position at Gutteridge's so that she could devote her attention to her family. From their marriage four children were born. We were not raised in wealth but food was never lacking and there were never debts of any kind. Our parents could have sent us to work when we were young but they preferred to have us study so that we could aspire to better employment opportunities. As a result, I am a full professor of Political Economics at the University of Rome; my brother Mario became an attorney; my sister Lia worked for various companies; and Paola worked with children.

While we were on vacation near Portici in the summer of 1939, my mother took my brother and me (six and four, respectively) to visit Mamma Santi. I think that she wanted to see Mamma Santi both to express her debt of gratitude and to have the pleasure of introducing her sons. I remember the maternal aspect of Mamma Santi as she sat in an armchair. I remember my mother's attitude full of respect and affection. Although she did not know the feeling of pride, my mother was truly happy to show that the education she had received at Casa Materna had borne good fruits. She returned as often as she could to visit Mamma Santi.

From my mother's stories it was clear to me that, from the first years of its life, Casa Materna was a place where children were loved and where they were given a complete education. In addition to being fed and educated, they received a profound religious education; they participated in field trips that put them in touch with nature; and they prepared theatrical productions that assisted in their civil education. It was truly an exceptional place and one in which children were carefully nurtured and grew into good citizens of society.

Note: Massimo Finoia died in June 2001 after a bout with cancer. It is very sad that he was not able to see the publication of this book. He was one of its most enthusiastic supporters.

Massimo Finoia
Casa Materna, June 1995
Photo: ©Fred Dole

CHAPTER 3

THE RISE OF FASCISM: 1920-1939

Black Shirts and Castor Oil

The 1920s began inauspiciously in Italy. It was time to pay the bill for World War I and the price included devaluation of the lira, inflation and widespread unemployment. These factors attracted Italians to the Fascist Party and its promises of domestic prosperity and international respect. In 1921, Mussolini's Fascist Party, now 150,000 strong, sent him to Parliament. On October 28, 1922, Mussolini and his men marched on Rome. The next day, King Victor Emanuel III appointed Mussolini as prime minister. Mussolini eliminated all political opponents of the Fascist Party. In 1929, he and the Pope signed the Lateran Agreements that created the sovereign Vatican state, made Catholicism the State religion, but put the Church in Italy under the control of Fascism. Mussolini's Fascist "Black Shirts" helped him govern with clubs and castor oil. (Dissenters were forced to swallow large quantities of castor oil which had a disastrous effect on their digestive systems). Italy became a totalitarian state.

The economic depression that hit the world in 1931 threatened Italy as well. In 1933, Adolph Hitler became chancellor of Germany and the country began to rearm. In 1935 and 1936, Mussolini sent troops to invade and conquer Ethiopia, and he supported Franco's Fascist takeover in Spain, alienating Italy's former allies, France and Great Britain. In 1939, Italy and Germany signed the Steel Pact (*Patto d'Acciaio*). Italy thus linked its fortunes to Hitler's "new" Germany.

Giorgio Quinzii and Giovanni Stoecklin entered Casa Materna in 1927 and in 1929, respectively. Giorgio left in 1930 while Giovanni remained a resident there until 1937, just before World War II broke out. Here they tell their stories.

Sunshine, Flowers, And Orange Trees

Giorgio Quinzii's Story

One day my father decided to go to South America to start a new life. He left behind my mother and six children. My mother had no means of support. She, therefore, placed two of my older siblings in a boarding school in Naples and took my younger brother, my sister, and me to Casa Materna. (I was the fourth child in the family.)

I don't remember my first day at Casa Materna but I clearly remember the three years that I lived there. I remember the splendid villa near the sea and the train that passed between the villa and the sea. In the first few months I was very homesick and I longed for freedom. I was then eight years old, and I dreamed about riding on that train in the direction of my house. Then Papà Santi, Mamma Santi, Fabio (I was his favorite), and Doctor Teofilo helped ease my pain. My boy friends, my girl friends (yes, there were girls at Casa Materna, too), and Signorina Chirico, the housemother, became my family.

I remember the school and the after-school sessions where I read many adventure books after doing my homework. The recreation period was spent in complete liberty within the grounds of the villa. I still remember the carob tree that I climbed as if it were a pirate ship. I remember our swims in the sea and the tennis games on the court between the porticos of the main building and the fountain.

I had many friends, in particular Giovanni Stoecklin [*Giovanni's story immediately follows Giorgio's. cfm*] and my friend Cioccolato (he was given this nickname because his mother always brought chocolate for all of us).

I left Casa Materna when I finished elementary school. I continued my studies and received a teaching certificate. I also began to study Colonial Sciences but I had to stop when World War II began and I was drafted. I survived four years of war in the Balkans and one year in a German concentration camp. I attribute my survival to the beneficial influence of Casa Materna on my character and on my body.

I am married and have three children. After I was married, I often took my wife and children to Casa Materna to stroll in the gardens of that wonderful villa. I still go back with my mind to Casa Materna and see my childhood there—full of sunshine, of the sea, of a garden full of flowers, of oranges, of many many orange trees, and of very very tall palm trees. Truly the three years that I spent at Casa Materna were among the most luminous of my childhood.

Little Soldiers

Giovanni Stoecklin's Story

My paternal grandfather was born in Switzerland (in Ettingen Basilea). As a young adult he went to Naples to set up a cotton factory. My father was born in Naples, but he was not an Italian citizen. He had Swiss citizenship like his father. He died when I was only eight months old, and he left my mother in a very precarious financial situation. She tried to find assistance in many different places but it was only the Swiss Consulate that came to her aid. Thanks to the Consulate's intervention, I was able to become a part of the great family of Casa Materna.

I entered Casa Materna in 1929 at the age of six. That day is as clear in my mind as if it were yesterday. I remember watching my mother walk away as she cried inconsolably. I myself didn't cry but I remember feeling very lost as I gazed at the children around me, so many children, big and small, boys and girls. I was overwhelmed with confusion. But I gradually became adjusted to my new life, and I stayed at Casa Materna for eight years.

Life was carefully regulated with precise hours for everything.

We were like little soldiers. Our daily schedule was prayer, breakfast, school, lunch, recreation, study, dinner, and prayer. We were very fortunate to have a vast play area just outside the door to the dining room. And we were able to take walks within the grounds of that wonderful villa.

Sunday was the most wonderful day of the week. The lunch was more varied and more substantial. Sometimes we even had dessert. But Sunday was especially wonderful because many of the parents would come to visit their children, and they would always bring a special treat, according to their financial abilities. Actually they would sometimes take food out of their own mouths in order to buy something delicious to give to their children. And we never lacked an appetite. We were always as hungry as bear cubs because of the good air at Casa Materna and because we burned up lots of calories. The parents and relatives would come on Sundays and stay from 4 to 8. Then we all went to the religious service in the chapel of Casa Materna that was almost always conducted by Papà Santi himself.

In the summer we had access to our own beach. There were two paths down to the ocean, one for the boys and the other for the girls who were always accompanied by their housemother. How long we were allowed to stay in the water was determined by our age. Some of the children were able to leave Casa Materna in the summer. I myself went to Switzerland every August. The Swiss Consulate arranged these trips so that I would become familiar with my native country. Host families would take me in. I am still in contact with many of these families today.

I had good days at Casa Materna but I also had bad ones. The bad days were frequently my fault because I was a restless child and I was, therefore, often punished. I will never forget the time I really received a paddling. I had climbed up on one of the many statues in the garden and risked pulling it down on top of me. Needless to say, I never went near a statue again.

I sometimes felt sad at the end of the day if I had quarreled with a friend, if I was sick and alone without my mother's comforting presence, or, if looking out the front gate, I saw people walking along Corso Garibaldi and longed to be free as they were. But I always received so much affection from Papà Santi and from the other members of his family. I will always remember this.

I attended all of the elementary school grades at Casa Materna and then a few years at the Industrial Institute nearby which I did not find much to my liking. I left Casa Materna when I was 14 years old. It was wonderful to return to my family. I continued my education but not at an industrial institute; I switched to accounting, a field in which I then worked happily until my retirement a few years ago. I worked in a private company owned by one of my half brothers.

In my heart I have a great deal of nostalgia for Casa Materna. I have mentioned people who are no longer living but their presence is indelible in my mind, and we are united in memory and prayer. Casa Materna had a very positive influence on my life.

Giovanni Stoecklin and Giorgio Quinzii
Casa Materna, summer 1995
Photo: © Fred Dole

CHAPTER 4

WORLD WAR II AND RECOVERY: 1940-1949

War, Peace and A Constitution

Italy entered World War II with Germany on June 10, 1940. Once again, the country was completely unprepared: Italian troops were ill equipped and were easily defeated in Russia and Africa. The war turned for Italy in 1943 when the Allied troops invaded Sicily on July 10. Two weeks later, King Victor Emmanuel III had Mussolini arrested. "Il Duce" escaped and fled to northern Italy where he formed a new "Fascist Republic."

In September 1943 the Allies invaded mainland Italy at Salerno just south of Naples and suffered terrible losses at the hands of the Germans. Italy withdrew from the war and became a war zone. German troops occupied the cities and countryside north of Rome, and Allied soldiers fought German troops in the south.

Italian civilians formed a resistance movement with the help of American and British troops. By war's end, 55,000 Italian partisans were dead and another 20,000 wounded. One of the most remarkable resistance battles took place in Naples in September 1943 when Neapolitan street children (in Italian *scugnizzi*) joined forces with housewives, grandparents, and other ordinary citizens to fight the Germans. Armed with only Molotov cocktails, old rifles, stones and broomsticks, the Neapolitans sabotaged German tanks and infantry for four days until they drove the enemy out of their city.

For nearly two years Italian partisans and Allied soldiers fought the Germans in Italy. In June 1944 the Allies entered Rome. Ten months later, Italian partisans captured Mussolini while he was trying to flee Italy. They executed him on April 28, 1945. The next month Germany surrendered. The war in Europe was over.

On June 2, 1946 Italy held a referendum to decide whether it would remain a constitutional monarchy or become a republic. The republic won by 2 million votes. In 1947 an elected assembly approved a new constitution that gave Italy a parliamentary government and women the right to vote. The first elections, held in 1948, brought to power a new party, the Christian Democrats, which governed Italy for nearly 50 years until 1995. The new parliament then elected Italy's first president, Enrico De Nicola.

Also in 1948, Italy joined the Marshall Plan and received massive aid that helped Italians rebuild their country. The next year, Italy joined the North Atlantic Treaty Organization (NATO) and took its place again among the Western allies now engaged in the Cold War with the Soviet Union.

Many families took their children to Casa Materna as a direct result of the misfortunes of the war. Giuseppe Abbellito, Giuseppe Sfameli, and Luigi Di Somma were three of these children.

Powdered Milk, Powdered Peas, and Powdered Eggs

Giuseppe Abbellito's Story

The war years represent a black period for my family. My father was an entrepreneur, the owner of four large colonial bars in Piazza San Ferdinando in Naples. [*A colonial bar was a cafe and pastry shop combined. cfm*] We were plunged into poverty when the Allied bombing destroyed these bars. After this disaster I was forced to go to Casa Materna. I entered Casa Materna twice. The first time was with two older sisters, Carmela and Rita, in 1943 before the German Occupation. The Santi family had to leave the Home when the Germans arrived and occupied Naples. They took many of the children with them to a village south of Naples. After the arrival of the Americans in 1945, they were able to return to Casa Materna. I returned to Casa Materna with my younger sister Maria in 1945 after the Americans arrived and I stayed until 1956.

I completed elementary school and junior high school at Casa Materna. Then I went to Istituto Luigi Petriccione, a professional school which was located near the Home. I would leave for school in the morning and return to Casa Materna in the evening.

Immediately after the war, life at the Home was difficult. We suffered from hunger. I remember that the Santis had a very tough job feeding 500 children, but everyone always sat down to three meals a day. This was due in large part to the assistance of the Americans who donated many food items such as powdered milk, powdered peas, and powdered eggs. For breakfast we had powdered or fresh milk. For lunch, the biggest meal of the day, we had soup and pasta for the first course and canned American beef and yellow Dutch cheese for the second. One of my very special memories is eating a small piece of bread spread with peanut butter for our afternoon snack. I still love peanut butter. As a special treat for me, my wife will look for peanut butter for me. Although it is hard to find in Italy, she sometimes finds it at the supermarket or sometimes we can get it at the NATO store.

The internal life at Casa Materna was highly regulated. We went to school in the mornings, and we worked a little in the afternoons. We also played a lot. We had a soccer team. I was the goalie and talented enough so that no one ever took this position away from me.

My most memorable experience was Casa Materna's U.S. choir tour. I was about 17 years old at the time. We sailed across the Atlantic on the Cristoforo Colombo. When the captain of the ship heard about our presence on board, he invited us to come to the First Class dining room for our meals and asked us to sing at dinner. We were the main attraction of the ship. The crossing lasted six days, and for six days we sang for the passengers of the ship.

The tour throughout the United States was really wonderful for us kids. We found singing fun, and we did it with a certain amount of professionalism. On some days we gave more than two concerts. Truthfully, singing for two hours with no music is hard work. But, wherever we went, we received thunderous applause, and, therefore, it was fun for us.

We had two changes of costume. We had blue outfits that we wore for the classic songs in the first part of the program. Then we wore traditional Neapolitan clothes when we sang

Neapolitan songs and danced the Tarantella. The Neapolitan songs were very popular, especially "O Marinariello." Everywhere we went, we had overwhelming success, and the media at the time always reported that the choir of young Italians did itself proud.

In Italy we began to see television around the end of 1956, but we had only one channel with very limited programming (a few evening hours). In the U.S. we saw television for the first time with several channels. But not only did we watch television. We were on television! In 1956 there was a famous TV show called "The Home of Arlene Francis." Our choir and the Vienna Choir Boys sang on one of these programs.

We never stayed in hotels because we were invited to stay with American families, friends of Casa Materna. These families extended their hospitality and during the day took us around to see all of the interesting sights in their cities. We went to see parks, zoos, ice skating performances, and other things like this. We then began our return trip, singing again in the same churches across the country and departing from New York aboard the Conte Biancamano.

Going to America was like going from a dark room to an illuminated one. We returned with many wonderful memories of our American friends but the return was bitter. In 1956 Italy was a country undergoing reconstruction. We went from a life of luxury and well being in the U.S. to our lives of want in Italy. As the Italian saying goes, we went "dalle stelle alle stalle" (from the stars to the horse stables).

When I finished my studies in 1960, I got a position with the local Cumana & Circumvesuviana Railroad. I worked as a train conductor for 10 years. Then I became depot supervisor and finally an office worker.

I have a wife and two adult children. My son Giovanni works in the field of electronics, is married, and has one son. My daughter worked as a bookkeeper until she was married.

Let me say something about politics. Unfortunately, because of my line of work, I became a member of the Communist CGL union and of the Communist Party. I then became the secretary of one of the cells of the Party. Therefore, when I applied for a visa to travel to the U.S. in 1957, my application was refused. Then in the years 1963-66 union members were persecuted in Italy. Every time there was a strike, the police came to my house; every time there was a meeting, the police chief came to interrogate me.

However, my conviction has always been that as long as it was a struggle for human rights, I wanted to be counted in. If the purpose is to give well-being to the various generations in the future, I am for it. It doesn't matter to me if I am on the Left or on the Right as long as the goal is human rights. Here in Italy we really suffered a lot before becoming a democratic country.

Giuseppe Abbellito
Casa Materna, summer 1995
Photo: ©Fred Dole

Stealing For Peanuts

Giuseppe Sfameli's Story

I was born in Naples in 1934, the second of four sons. Before the Second World War we were a very religious Catholic family, and we were all actively involved in the life of our church.

Then the war broke out, and our travails began. My father had been working as a tram driver but during the war there were few riders in war-torn Naples so he was laid off. The immediate result of this situation was that we did not have enough to eat. As a matter of fact, my brother Virgilio died of starvation at the age of nine. At this point my father decided to take us away from Naples to a small town in Basilicata called Bargianna where more food would be available. We were warmly welcomed there and felt at home.

As soon as the war was over, we returned to Naples. My father did not have a job, and so again we did not have enough food. We were forced to eat whatever we found, even garbage that we found on the street. It was at this time that I learned how to steal. I did not go to school because the schools had not been reopened yet. My friends and I spent our days stealing wood from buildings and then selling it to an old woman who in return gave us nuts to eat.

I didn't really like this kind of life. I was humiliated and also afraid. Finally one day I said to my mother, "Please, Mamma. I don't want to live in the streets anymore. I want to be put into a home for children." At first my mother was opposed to this idea but I convinced her that it would be better for me. She decided to go to the nuns at St. Peter's. These nuns knew her well. However, they told her that they did not have a place for me. Then we went to the Salesians. The director of the school received us cordially but he told my mother, "I am sorry, Signora Sfameli. We cannot take him."

My father then began to drive the tram again occasionally. One day he heard about Casa Materna from one of his passengers. He arrived home a very happy man that day and told my mother that he had found an institution for me. When she heard that it was a Protestant institution, she was not happy but she said, "Mamma mia, after all of our suffering, we are now going to go to the Inferno as well! All right! If my son is going to the Inferno, I am going to go, too!" This shows how great was her desire to help me.

Before taking me to Casa Materna, my mother made an enormous sacrifice and bought me a pair of new sandals. However, I almost immediately lost one of them while playing soccer with my friends. My mother did not become angry but simply said, "This means that Jesus Christ wants you to be barefooted!" She then bought me a pair of soldier's boots that were much too big for me but were cheap and then took me to Casa Materna.

Luisa Santi, the daughter of Papà and Mamma Santi, was the one who welcomed us on our first visit to Casa Materna. Seeing what a terribly agitated state we were in, she gently took my mother by the arm and told us not to worry. When her brother Fabio came to speak with us, my mother immediately said, "I have to leave my son here. His father, my husband, works only now and then. We have no money. I must appeal to your generosity." Fabio replied, "Don't worry. We will talk about that later." In truth he never again mentioned money; my family was never asked to pay anything to Casa Materna.

My first day at Casa Materna was very peaceful. I had no worries. I saw a world that was completely new, a reality that was beyond any of my dreams. Soon my brother Giorgio came to join me in this new world.

When the word got around that I had gone to a Protestant institution, the heavens opened up. The nun at St. Peter's who had said that she had no room for me suddenly changed her mind. "Where have you taken your son?" she asked my mother. "You have taken him to the Inferno! He will lose his soul. Go and get him immediately! We will take him!" The priest at St. George's also objected strenuously.

Signor Megnardini, the man who accepted much of my mother's embroidery work, was angry as well. He assembled a group of church women to meet with my mother. When they questioned her about what she had done, she calmly replied: "I know what I have done. I have taken this step. No one can make me turn back."

With so much hostile opposition, we all became Protestants. I must hasten to add, however, that today the relations between the Catholic and Protestant churches in Portici are excellent. We engage in many activities together. And, of course, most of the children at Casa Materna continue to be Catholic. The emphasis is on Christianity, not on a particular denomination. We do have some Muslim children and their religious beliefs are respected as well.

After leaving Casa Materna, I attended a mission school of the Church of Christ in Frascati, a Roman hill town, for three years. Students came to this school from all over Italy, many of whom were from Naples. I was taught how to prepare and deliver sermons and became a licensed lay preacher.

After I returned to Naples, I began to work as an insurance agent but the pay unfortunately was very poor. I then had the opportunity to obtain a position as a meter reader for the electric company. The problem was, however, that they wanted a deposit of 300,000 lire that I did not have. My father then asked Dr. Teofilo if he would make me a loan. Dr. Teofilo immediately exclaimed, "Anything for Geppino!" He had always thought of me as a real son. Without hesitation he gave me the money for the deposit so that I could obtain the position. And I still have the position today.

If, as a child, I had remained on the street, I would have continued my erratic life, and I would most likely have become mixed up in delinquency. Instead, I have had a happy life—a steady job and a wonderful family.

I am married and have three children, two daughters and one son. My son is 29 years old, is married, and has a two-year old son. He lives in Rovigo in northern Italy. He is an inspector for the Department of Finance. My older daughter lives in Caserta and is married to a man who is a computer programmer at the Bank of Naples. My younger daughter is 18 and still living at home.

I live about 200 meters from Casa Materna. Every day around dinner time I go over there. I spend some time with the children, I help with the daily service in the chapel, and then I stay for dinner. My wife knows where I am and doesn't complain. She understands that Casa Materna has remained my true home.

Giuseppe Sfameli
Casa Materna, summer 1995
Photo: ©Fred Dole

The Pots are Mine!

Luigi Di Somma's Story

My name is Luigi Francesco Scipione Di Somma. My parents had fourteen children, and I was the youngest. So I was Louis the 14th! My oldest sister and I are 24 years apart. We were born on the same day, September 19th! Four of my brothers have died, either because of the war or because of illness.

My oldest brother Angelo was a soldier in the Italian Army during World War II. The English took him prisoner and sent him to South Africa. The English treated the prisoners well, knowing that they would not run away because they were so far from Italy. Angelo worked in the fields and, while working, he met an English woman. He married her and never returned to Italy. Many Italian prisoners decided to stay there after the war.

My father died as a result of the war. He was an officer in an artillery division. He operated an anti-aircraft battery. One day a grenade exploded near him, and a piece of it went into his leg. Gangrene set in, and he died at the beginning of 1945. And so my mother became a widow. I was just six years old.

After my father's death we lived through a truly difficult period. No one could help us then because everyone was in the same boat. In that period of time it was taboo, especially in the South, for women to work outside of the home. My mother was, therefore, not able to feed all of her children. My brother Vincenzo almost died of starvation at the age of 15. He was so hungry that he used to steal food from a German camp nearby; needless to say, this was a highly risky endeavor.

My older sisters and one of my older brothers tried to help out with odd jobs but their help was not enough. And so my mother, overcome by discouragement because of the serious economic difficulties, decided to put some of us in institutions in order to lighten the load for the family. At this time my oldest sister Filomena married a Protestant man who knew the Santi family. He suggested that my mother speak with the Santis to see if they would take in two or three of the youngest children in our family.

My mother plucked up her courage and went with my sister and her husband to Portici to talk to the Santi family and to explain to them the desperate straits in which our family found itself. Papà and Mamma Santi, listening to the reasons she gave for her decision, understood well our difficult situation. They tried to make it clear to my mother that not even at Casa Materna was there enough food for all of the mouths that had to be fed, even with the help that arrived, thank God, from many foreign benefactors, especially the Americans.

But, in any case, Papà and Mamma Santi (whom I have always considered two angels sent to earth by God) didn't discourage my mother. In fact, they encouraged her by saying that God would provide for us as well just as He would provide for the other children at Casa Materna. Papà Santi always had faith and often he was heard saying, "Add another place at the table."

My brother Giulio, who was five years older than me, went to Casa Materna a few months before I did and stayed there for about seven years. I stayed for ten years from May 1946 to December 1956. My sister Bianca went for one year and Lucia for three months.

To tell you the truth, I cannot clearly remember my first day at Casa Materna because I was in a state of great confusion. I understood but dimly the reasons why I was being taken there, and I was very sad at the sudden separation from my mother and from the rest of my family. It was really quite traumatic for me. I felt very uncomfortable there among so many unfortunate children whom I did not yet know. It was a day that was anything but happy.

I remember very well that my mother, seeing me so miserable, tried to make me understand. She said that I would be well taken care of. I would grow up to be a well-mannered person, I would have the opportunity to study along with the other children, and I would be able to play with them as well. I would also feel happy to be near my brother Giulio. But, regardless of these words that encouraged me a bit, I was still sad and I didn't respond. Then I walked to the gate of Casa Materna with her. She hugged me and gave me a few coins and a few things to eat. It took many days for me to get used to my new situation but I gradually resigned myself to a new life so different from my life at home and I became a part of the great family formed by Papà and Mamma Santi.

Casa Materna was like a busy beehive. The Santi family, along with the staff and other supporters, had to work very hard to keep Casa Materna running. It was a tremendous job to take care of so many children, to feed them, to clothe them, to educate them, and to do all of the other necessary things. The discipline was strict, sometimes rather severe but it was necessary to educate so many boys and girls, to organize the many activities of our daily life—recreational opportunities, study periods, music lessons and practice, Bible studies, and Sunday School classes.

We were hungry in those years. There were 350 of us to feed. Imagine! And I must make it clear that the Santi family always ate the same things that we did. I remember that we older boys came up with some creative ways to satisfy our hunger.

Let me first tell you about the pots. One day it occurred to some of us that something always stuck to the bottoms of the large cooking pans. So we went to the kitchen to ask the cooks if we could eat what there was. They told us, "Sure! Scrape the bottoms of the pots and eat as much as you like. But you must wash the pots after you finish." We accepted these conditions willingly. This will give you an idea of how hungry we were!

But there wasn't enough to satisfy everyone in our group so we made a pact. Whoever woke up first in the morning would yell, "I get all of the pots!" and that person would have the right to scrape all of the pots that day. It was a competition. But there was one condition. No one could yell until the first light of day was seen. The first one to see the light could shout. We used to try to wake up by 4 in order to be first!

Any leftover bread was kept in a little room with bars on the door. It was later cut and moistened in water with laurel leaves, causing it to expand in size. Eating it filled us up and satisfied our hunger. We kids knew how to make this special bread. Sometimes in the afternoons, when the coast was clear, "little mice" would slip between the bars of the door into the pantry and steal some of the hard bread in order to make the special treat.

Then there were the powdered peas, ground peas, an American product. In water the peas expanded. I liked them then. Oh, what hunger will do! Today, however, if someone in my family so much as mentions powdered peas, I get the shivers! But we were among the lucky few who had these peas.

It was understandable at that time why we wanted to scrape pots or to squeeze through bars to get old, dry bread. Today it's hard to understand such things, at least in Italy. Perhaps not in the Third World. It seems incredible. But these memories remain, sad, yes, but still treasured memories.

I left Casa Materna in December of 1956 during the Christmas holidays. Since I had reached the age of sixteen, my mother explained to me that she needed my assistance at home. All of my brothers and sisters had married and left home and had to think about their own families. My mother had still not begun to receive her pension as a war widow and, therefore, she had no fixed regular income to support her.

I admit that, amidst the great joy of being able to return to my own home, I felt at the same time great sadness at leaving so many dear friends with whom I had grown up. What truly moved me was the fact that I felt as if they were truly my brothers. And to this day I maintain strong ties with several of them. I also felt great sadness at leaving the Santi family that had been the anchor of salvation in my life.

Every morning I went to school and earned a diploma with a specialization in industrial motors, and every afternoon I went to work in various garages in order to bring some money home. At the age of nineteen I was called up for my compulsory military service. For eighteen months I traveled over most of Italy, from Trapani to Trieste. When I returned home, the economic situation had not changed much.

At the age of 21 I met Angela who is now my wife. I have been very happy with her. We were married on June 18, 1961, and we have five children, four daughters and one son. Our son is now fourteen and is in his first year in a high school which specializes in sciences. I often talk to my son about Casa Materna, about my childhood there.

He treasures these memories in his heart. My son's name is Giulio Riccardo. He carries the name of the father Giulio that I never knew and the name of Papà Riccardo Santi who became my true father.

When I have the opportunity, I preach in the daily services in the chapel. I am also a member of the church council. I participate in planning and teaching the lessons for the Sunday School. This involvement makes me happy because I can be of service to Casa Materna. Casa Materna is still in my heart along with all of those people who work for this great work of God.

Luigi Di Somma
Casa Materna, summer 1995
Photo: ©Fred Dole

CHAPTER 5

THE WONDER YEARS: 1950-1969

The Economic Boom of the Fabulous Years

Italy prospered in the decades that followed World War II. These years were known as the "anni favolosi" (*the wonder years*) because they were marked by growth in foreign trade and domestic industry. Most of this well-being, however, was confined to the regions north of Rome. For the people of southern Italy, life continued as it had for centuries, marked by poverty, unemployment, and corruption.

In 1957, Italy joined the European Common Market, giving its industries new opportunities for trade and its needy southerners new countries in which they could seek work and a better life than Italy could offer them.

Casa Materna had many mouths to feed in this period of time but a great deal of assistance came from outside of Italy, especially from the United States. The fifteen residents who tell their stories in this chapter remember days of relative plenty and good employment opportunities after their Casa Materna education.

Standing Up to Mussolini

Giuseppe Zampino's Story

I was born in Macchia Valfortore, a small village of Molise, a region in the heart of southern Italy. This area was a depressed area when I was born and it is still considered an economically-depressed area today. The only activity is agriculture, one that does not offer great opportunities for social evolution.

My father was a carpenter, and my mother worked in the fields. They were both Protestants. The situation was very difficult for them in a small village where everyone else was Catholic. They were watched with suspicion, and people kept their distance from them. My father always said that some day the Catholics would understand the Protestants. The situation did not begin to change until the election of Pope John Paul II.

Since our village was very poor and did not offer many educational opportunities, my parents decided to send me away to school. My father knew the Santi Family, and they accepted me at Casa Materna. Papà Santi actually came to Macchia Valfortore himself to get me and take me to Casa Materna. I remember that the first person that I met when I arrived there was Mamma Santi. She was so kind that I felt as if I had known her for a long time. She offered me a piece of candy and then introduced me to some other boys who were living there.

I kept in touch with my parents by correspondence. Once a year they came to Casa Materna to visit me. Unfortunately in those years the opportunities to travel were very limited, especially because of the scant economic resources.

Papà and Mamma Santi had to struggle against many powerful outside forces. Not only did they have to fight against local public opinion as Protestants were viewed with suspicion and animosity, but they also had to fight against the national Fascist government as well. Mussolini was closely connected to the Catholic Church and looked with disfavor upon Protestants. He actually tried to close Casa Materna because it was a Protestant home. But Papà Santi never felt intimidated. As a matter of fact, he confronted the Fascists and, with love and religious persuasion, he convinced them that the work of Casa Materna was a benefit for everyone, especially for poor and abandoned children (as it still is and thus this great story continues). The Santis won the battle, but the time of Fascist rule was a very difficult period for them and the supporters of Casa Materna.

Many children lived at Casa Materna. It was in our interest to be united and to get along well with each other and we succeeded in this very well. My first and best friend was Paolo Chianese, a boy much older than I was. He was 18 while I was just nine. Adapting to my new life at Casa Materna was a bit hard, and I immediately saw in Paolo an older brother who could guide me with love and with passion to surmount the difficulties.

I remember two other friends in particular. One is Luigi Di Somma who is still my great friend. [*See Luigi di Somma's story above. cfm*] He was a boy who always had both feet on the ground and never did crazy things. Salvatore Avella, on the other hand, was a very exuberant and noisy type. He was lots of fun and was a little crazy but a very good person. He also helped me a lot. Unfortunately he lost his hand while in the military. A bomb exploded in his hand. He's now working in a bank.

I received a diploma in metal finishing from an institute near Casa Materna, and then joined the Italian Navy. Pastor Emanuele organized a farewell party for me on my last day. In a little ceremony he said some kind words about me, and I felt very important. He concluded by expressing his hope that I would always walk in the way of our Lord. Then we were all offered some sweets. We rarely had sweets at Casa Materna, usually only at Christmas and Easter, because money was scarce. This party was very special indeed, a moving experience.

After about thirty months, I decided not to follow a military career and left the Navy to find work in my field. My specialization was very much in demand and, through a friend who was living in Switzerland, I found out about employment opportunities there. I went to work in a large factory of surgical instruments near Bern for about 8 months. I was able to complete my practical training in this way. I then returned to Italy and worked for a company near Caserta for a year before being hired by Silenia. I have spent thirty years with Silenia and am currently the head of their electrolysis treatment division. I am about to retire because anyone who has been with Silenia for thirty years can retire five years in advance.

I married a woman who had also lived at Casa Materna. We were there at the same time but we had not really noticed each other. After I completed my military service, I went to visit the Santis one day and I saw her there. We became friends and then we were married. She is currently employed as a secretary. We have three children. Marco has a diploma in electronics and he repairs video tape recorders, radios, and hi-fi sets. Donatella teaches Italian in Casa Materna's elementary school and also studies at the University of Naples. My youngest son Fabio is a high school student.

The lives of my children have been much more comfortable than mine was even though they have the misfortune of living in a time of global economic recession. I think that we are in this recession because we have been involved in a frenetic race to produce. We need to slow down. We have forgotten that there are trees, that there are flowers here in Italy.

I don't know how my life would have turned out without Casa Materna. I often go back to Casa Materna on Sundays. I live about five or six kilometers away, near Villa Betania. [*Villa Betania is the hospital established by Doctor Teofilo. cfm*]When I am there, wherever I stop, in any spot, I remember something. For example, if I look at the bushes, I think about the times we would have to clean the grounds. Someone would always run off and hide to get out of doing the work! Casa Materna gave me a great deal. It shaped me as a man. It introduced me to Christ who has been the real guide of my life. I was given the possibility to study. I was able to see the United States and other places in Europe.

Giuseppe Zampino
Casa Materna, summer 1995
Photo: ©Fred Dole

The Whipped Cream Fiasco

Franco "Pippo" Maccarrone's Story

My parents were Sicilian but immediately after they were married, they left Messina to go north. My father was a fisherman. He decided to move because the sea on the Ligurian coast was richer in fish, and it was easier to sell fish there because it was a wealthier area economically. My mother was a housewife. I was born in Sanremo.

When the Germans abandoned Liguria in 1945 at the arrival of the Allied Forces, they took my father prisoner and carried him off to Austria. After his release, he decided to return to Sicily. I was not quite two at the time. A year later my mother died at the age of 31. For a while I went back and forth between the home of my maternal grandmother in Messina and my father's home in Sant'Alessio Siculo. Then I was taken to Casa Materna. This was the historical post-war period. In Sicily (and actually in all of Italy) even those who were lucky enough to have jobs were barely able to survive.

My memory is a little fuzzy about my first day at Casa Materna. I remember a certain uneasiness in finding myself in the midst of more than 300 children who spoke in a dialect different from mine. They spoke the Neapolitan dialect rather than the Sicilian one. And it was the first time I had ever been without a member of my family close by. I felt a little bit reassured when the few hymns that I knew were sung.

When I was around thirteen or fourteen, Signora Livia gave me the responsibility for the keys to the kitchen. It was a position of great trust. Looking back, I wonder how I was able to do this job. The baker would arrive in his horse-drawn cart with bags full of Neapolitan bread. He would come into the kitchen and put the bags on the scales. I had to check the weight, and on the basis of that, I had to estimate—in a few minutes only—how much bread we would need for the following day.

This was a big responsibility but we never ran short of bread. If I calculated wrong, it was always on the side of too much bread.

And if there was too much bread, we had to eat hard bread. Actually there was always hard bread because I ordered bread so that we would never run out. In one corner of the dining room there was a little table where the boys took turns cutting the bread. [*The boys no longer cut the bread. According to the Director, the boys of today are not very careful, and they are no longer assigned this task. cfm*] The bread was then put in little baskets and distributed to all of the children, to the Santi family, and to the guests who always ate with the children.

One of my favorite memories is what we can call "The Whipped Cream Fiasco." One day a van arrived with a big barrel full of whipped cream. I filled many small bowls with it and put a bowl on each table. Each bowl had enough whipped cream so that each child would have one or two spoonsful. And then—do you know what I did? I took one of the bowls and I hid it. The whipped cream was such a temptation for me! I wanted to save a whole bowl that I could eat all by myself after dinner. Signor Franceschini who was the administrator at that time always used to say to me, "Enter the kitchen singing but leave it whistling." In other words, "Take what you want but don't bring anything out with you."

So I hid the bowl. Since there was a lot of whipped cream in it, I decided that I had better not eat any dinner. All of the children ate dinner while I patiently fasted, dreaming of my hidden bowl of whipped cream. After dinner some of the boys stayed to clean the tables. While they were doing this, I went into the back and started to eat my bowl of whipped cream. First one spoonful, then another, then another and then I couldn't eat anymore! Whipped cream is very filling. I got to the fourth spoonful and I just couldn't go on. So I called the boys cleaning the tables for help and in two minutes they had finished the bowl! That evening I had eaten less than usual!

Let me tell you about another strong memory that I have. One day in 1958 I created a big stir because I had a very high fever. The nurse in Casa Materna's infirmary was very frightened. Dr. Teofilo was working outside of Casa Materna and could not be located right away. Somehow one of my American sailor friends found out that I was sick, and he called the doctor on the aircraft carrier the Forrestal. Someone else called the doctor of the Waldesian Church. Therefore, I was visited by a host of doctors. The first one to arrive was the doctor from the Forrestal. Then the doctor from the Waldesian Church arrived followed by Dr. Teofilo. The last to see me was the doctor who made the rounds every morning at Casa Materna. With all of this medical attention, I soon recovered!

The last year that I lived at Casa Materna I went to a school outside with some other boys. Before leaving every morning we stopped in to see Papà and Mamma Santi. We would say a prayer together and then go on to the school in San Giovanni a Teduccio.

I left Casa Materna at the wishes of my Uncle Rosario Salviera, one of my mother's brothers. I remember that I was in the music room when Pastor Emanuele called me to his study to tell me that I would be leaving Casa Materna with a friend of my uncle's. I returned to Sicily and continued to study. First I attended and graduated from a technical high school in Messina. Then I received a degree in Biological Sciences at the University of Messina. I also attended a Waldesian theology school but I left to go to Sardinia to teach. Since 1985 I have been living in Rome where I teach natural sciences, chemistry, and geology in high school.

I am married and we have three children, Dino, Davide, and Irene. My wife teaches English in a commercial high school. We all attend the Waldesian Church in Piazza Cavour where my children attend Sunday School.

While at Casa Materna I always had before my eyes the example and presence of a family devoted to the education of children. At that time in Italy the school-attendance law existed only on paper and not in practice as it does today. I received a global education: school, music, cultural visits (Herculaneum, Pompeii, the theater, etc.), responsibility for the kitchen, experience in electrical work, hair cutting (the older boys cut the younger boys' hair), and house painting. I learned how to be lighthearted, to be loyal to others, to develop friendships, to have fun, to study, to have faith. I am grateful to Casa Materna for all the people I met there and for all the things that I learned.

Note: Franco Maccarrone died in the spring of 2002 after a brief bout with cancer, leaving behind his wife and three small children. As in the case of Massimo Finoia, it is sad that he was unable to see the publication of this book.

Franco Maccarrone with wife and sons
Rome, summer 1995
Photo: Family Maccarrone

A Visit from Gregory Peck

Luigi Corti's Story

I remember very clearly the day my uncle came to my house and announced that Casa Materna had a place for me. He put me on his motorcycle and took me there. I was seven years old at that time and was living alone with my mother. My father had died a few years before. How I cried when I had to leave my mother! My first day at Casa Materna was, therefore, a very sad day for me. I adjusted quite quickly, however, with the help of my older brother who had already gone to live there. I have both happy and sad memories of Casa Materna but most of them are happy ones.

I remember that all of the girls lived upstairs in the main building. The boys who lived downstairs were strictly forbidden to go up there but sometimes we would dash upstairs to whisper a few words to some girl. If we were caught, our housemother Signorina Poli gave us a severe paddling. She did not want us to go near the girls. We also sometimes tried to talk to the girls at mealtime. But it was next to impossible because the separation of the sexes was enforced as strictly in the dining hall as it was in the living quarters.

I remember that one day in 1958 or 1959 some famous American actors visited Casa Materna. One of them was Gregory Peck. And then the actor of that famous film "Bus Stop." I don't remember his name. They came because they had heard about Casa Materna from Pastor Emanuele in the States. They ate with us in the dining hall, and some of our parents also came to join us on this occasion.

While I was at Casa Materna, a boy died in an accident. He was sliding down the banister in the school building and fell down the stairwell from the fifth floor to the first. I used to slide down this banister myself because it was shiny and slippery. Once I fell off near the bottom and broke some of my teeth. I was lucky.

A year after I left, my friend Domenico was killed. While he was playing soccer one day, one of the boys kicked the ball over the wall and onto the railroad tracks. Domenico jumped over the wall to get it and was hit by a train. He was about fourteen.

I am currently working for a medical laboratory. I sell microscopes, reactors, alcohol, and other medical products. I am married and have one son who is 21. He is studying economics at the university now but he may not have the patience to finish. He has earned a diploma that qualifies him to be a computer data entry operator, and he is eager to find a steady job. He has already been engaged for four years. But he's not ready to get married yet because he is too young.

When I got married, most young men got married at 26 or 27. Now they take their time and get married at 30, 31, or even 32. Everyone completes the compulsory number of school years, and many go on to college; therefore, they get married later. Young people also wait longer nowadays because of the difficulty of finding a house and the difficulty of finding a job.

As my wife will tell you, my memories of Casa Materna are very positive.

Note: Luigi arrived at the interview with his wife. He was happy to talk about his memories of Casa Materna. His wife mentioned that Luigi was very proud of Casa Materna and soon after they became engaged, he took her there to show her where he had spent his formative years.

Luigi Corti
Casa Materna, summer 1995
Photo: ©Fred Dole

Growing Up in Paradise

Ciro Arienzo's Story

My father left my mother with seven children when he went to live with another woman. My mother had to work because the money she received from him was not enough to support our big family. She earned money by taking care of the children of one of her sisters who worked in a tobacco factory. My second brother helped by working as a photographer. Another brother worked sporadically in a pizzeria in Naples. One of my sisters learned how to sew very well and went to work as a seamstress. My other sisters could not sew and so they stayed at home. My oldest brother left home when he got a job with the railroad and immediately got married.

I was the youngest, the seventh child. My mother could not provide for me so she took me to Casa Materna. I was seven years old at the time, and I can still remember clearly the day she took me there. We went on foot from Bella Vista to Portici. My mother walked the entire way in silence. It was very painful for us to say good-bye when we arrived at Casa Materna.

My mother would come to visit me every Thursday and every Sunday. She always brought me fresh fruit—cherries and strawberries, for example—because she knew that I liked fruit a lot. She was an exceptional woman, very charitable and very loving with all of her children. When I left Casa Materna in August for the summer holidays, I would often go to visit my father because I did not see him during the year.

My fondest memory is my mother's excitement when I performed in the opera La Traviata at one of the anniversary celebrations. When I appeared on stage as the soloist, I saw her telling everyone around her that I was her son. Her pride made me very happy.

Another favorite memory is the incident of the missing shoes. One night another boy and I were unable to sleep because of the constant meowing of some cats in the garden under our window. We decided to get rid of these annoying animals. We grabbed the first shoes that we could lay our hands on and hurled them at the cats in the garden below. The next morning several boys were surprised to find that their shoes were missing!

During the summer each one of us was given a job to help keep Casa Materna beautiful. I was assigned to work in the orchard. I liked working there because I love lemons, especially the green ones. When I had finished working, Signora Maria would give me all of the lemons that I could eat. I could usually eat two but not more!

After I had completed one year of high school at a school near Casa Materna, Dr. Teofilo decided that it was time for me to return home to my mother. The first few days after my departure from Casa Materna were hard because life outside was so different. And I must admit that I had some regrets about leaving Casa Materna, especially leaving my friends.

I was able to continue my studies because of the financial assistance of my English sponsor. Without his help I would have had to start working at the age of 15 because we did not have any money at home. After I finished my studies, my sponsor helped me find a job in a textile factory in Manchester, England. I worked there for three years. This period was a very enriching one for me. I found great satisfaction in my work. Living alone I developed a very strong character. I was also able to learn English well because I took courses for foreigners in the evenings after work. I really liked the beautiful green English parks very much. I also liked the English way of life. I must confess that I still feel homesick for that life at times.

When I returned to Italy, I worked in a metal factory in Naples for a year and a half. Then I got a job with the railroad in 1971. I've been with the railroad ever since—22 years now. I've grown old working on the railroad!

I am married to a Neapolitan woman and we have two daughters. The older one is studying law at the university. The younger one graduated from a high school for the arts and is now taking a course in theater. She wants to become an actress but in Naples, as in most places, it is not easy to get into this field. I now have a house in Herculaneum that my sponsor helped me to buy. I was so fortunate with my sponsor!

I was named after San Ciro, the patron saint of Portici. Although I lived in England for a few years, Portici is my real home and Casa Materna is still very much a part of my life. I learned many things at Casa Materna. One of the most important was an appreciation for the beauty of creation because the environment of Casa Materna was so green, so beautiful and so tranquil. Living there was like being in paradise! In Naples, even in our residential areas, there is very little green and there are no parks where children can play. Casa Materna was a wonderful place for a child to grow up. Even now, when I want to find peace, I spend entire days at Casa Materna. I walk through the main gate and am immediately in another world. The separation between Casa Materna and the external environment is total.

The most important lesson I learned at Casa Materna was to love your neighbor. When I go home after work at night, I always kiss everyone in my house, whether they are relatives or not. I learned to show my affection for others at Casa Materna. Casa Materna is still a place full of affection. I like to go there because, as soon as I arrive, I am surrounded by all of the children who hug me and kiss me. Friends and strangers alike receive these spontaneous displays of affection. And I am always warmly welcomed by Signora Livia and invited to lunch.

I am still very tied to Casa Materna. Whenever I receive an invitation for a special event like the anniversary celebration or a Christmas program, I try to go. I like attending these events because I enjoy meeting many of my old friends.

Piazza San Ciro, Portici

A Born Teacher

Antonietta Romano's Story

My parents were Sicilians who had moved to Naples just before I was born. My father died when I was very young, perhaps only eight or nine months old. My mother did not remarry and then, when I was six, she died, too. My relatives then looked for an institution where I could get a good education and also feel the warmth of a family. I think my aunt knew some people at NATO who told her about Casa Materna. That's why I was taken there.

I don't remember my first day at Casa Materna. But I have many other memories. My memories of Casa Materna are very vivid. And every time I go back there, I relive all of my experiences. When I was there, there were many more residential children than there are now. There were also day children who came from Naples to attend the school at Casa Materna. These children stayed for lunch but they didn't eat with us. There were so many resident children that there was no extra room in our dining hall so they ate in a dining room in the school building. I think that they were given the first course, either pasta or soup. Then they ate sandwiches that they had brought from home.

And the sea! How wonderful it was to have our own beach and to be able to swim every day for three months of the year. I learned to swim there at the age of six. The water was so beautiful. I have had a great passion for the sea ever since. I love the sea.

When I left Casa Materna at the age of 18, I went to Switzerland. I made the trip with Pastor Emanuele, Signora Livia, and Dr. Santi. I had been invited to the home of a Swiss family that I had met during one of their visits to Casa Materna. I had become friends with the daughter, and she had invited me to visit her in Switzerland.

My "vacation" in Switzerland lasted three years. The plan was that I would stay for a few months but I had already thought about staying there. I was really happy there, really happy. I have wonderful memories of those years. I was in Neuchatel in the French part of Switzerland. I immediately started studying French because I had not studied it in school. As soon as I had mastered the language, when I spoke it quite well, I enrolled in a nursing course.

Then one summer I returned to Naples for a vacation. Something very important happened during this visit: I met my future husband. I returned to Switzerland but not alone. When I met him, I told him that I would only be in Naples for a short time and then I would return to Switzerland. He immediately said, "I will come with you. No problem!" So he did and we stayed for about one year. He didn't like the life there, however. He continued to feel like an immigrant. I didn't. I really felt at home there. I had taught him a little French before we left Naples. Therefore, when we went there, he could understand and speak a little. So it wasn't so much the language as the way of life that bothered him. He is a true Neapolitan and just couldn't adapt to his new life there. So we returned to Naples.

My husband and I have three children, a son and two daughters. We live right in the center of Naples, Via Chaia and Via Roma near the Royal Palace. This is a rather sad time for my son Antonio. He has graduated from the university but he cannot find work. Times are difficult now in Italy. He is doing occasional jobs. Yesterday, for example, he went out in a boat with a friend to catch mussels that they then sold. He does what he can. Paola is a secretary. But she also works only occasionally. She substitutes for secretaries who are ill and don't go to work. She had previously been a salesperson in a clothing store. Zitti is now studying to become a tourist guide. It's a five-year course. She wanted to become a secretary but there is not much work in this area.

I have been giving private lessons for fifteen years. I now work only with elementary school children. I don't work any set number of hours per week because it depends on how much homework the children have. They can come to my house between 2:30 in the afternoon and 8 or 9 o'clock in the evening. It's important that these children feel that they are good students and that they can succeed. Before coming to me they have problems, they are unable to write well. Then gradually during the year, they learn and then they begin to love school more.

It's work that I love to do. It reminds me of my experience at Casa Materna. When I was older, I was always called to substitute when one of the teachers was absent. I also helped a lot in the nursery because at that time there were many little children. There were about twenty children between the ages of three and five. I think that the directors saw how much I liked children. They chose me from among many girls (and there really were many of us at that time). Their intuition about me was very good! My love for children is my lasting legacy from my days at Casa Materna.

Note: Antonietta Romano arrived for the interview with her two lovely daughters. They knew all of her stories about Casa Materna because she had joyously shared them with her family over the years.

Gardens of Casa Materna
Photo: Casa Materna Archives

A New Life in Switzerland

Yvonne Polizzi Fargnoli's Story

When I was seven, my mother died and my aunt took me to
Casa Materna. I remember my first day at Casa Materna very clearly.
I arrived in the afternoon on October 8, 1952. The children were
just leaving the school, and my aunt said to me, "Look at how
many children there are!" I was happy but at the same time I felt a
stab in my heart, remembering that I would never see my mother
again. That night at dinner I cried because I was so sad, but the
older girls comforted me. And thus began my stay at Casa Materna
which lasted for eleven years.

I have many memories. Singing was a big part of our life there.
Casa Materna developed in me a great love for music. To this day I
still love to sing. Our choir was very special. We learned lots of
songs, and we spent many happy hours singing. I remember how

we always sang with great pleasure on our bus outings and how we were dismissed from school early when visitors from Switzerland were expected so that we could sing for them.

I loved the embroidering classes after school as well as the sewing classes. The girls spent a lot of time sewing the smocks for school and other things. Later on I was in charge of the smallest children in the nursery along with Antonietta Romano. *[See Antonietta's story above. cfm]*

All of us enjoyed our frequent visits to the U.S. Navy ships in the port of Naples very much.

In every family the children eventually leave home. I left Casa Materna because I was 18 years old and the Santis felt that it was time for me to try my wings. The Santis decided that I would go to Switzerland. I spent my last day just like the other days. I took care of the little ones in the nursery with Antonietta who was also going to Switzerland. We took the children to the beach and to dinner. We took care of them all day as always. Then we shortened the clothes that Signora Luisa had brought us from America that we would put on the next morning when we left for Switzerland.

Everything seemed normal that day but inside I felt a great joy thinking about my departure for Switzerland and a great sadness at the same time because I was leaving the place where I had grown up, the place that had provided me with everything I needed as a child. On July 18th, 1963 Antonietta and I left for Switzerland, accompanied by Dr. Teofilo and Signora Livia. They took me to the home of one of the sponsors of Casa Materna. I never felt abandoned because they wrote to me often, and I frequently wrote to them as well.

I went to the French part of Switzerland. I had a lot of difficulty at the beginning because I did not know a word of French. I was lucky, however, because the woman I lived with and two of her five daughters spoke Italian. They helped me to learn French quite quickly.

But at first I did not like Switzerland at all. I did not like the French language. I didn't like the mountains because they seemed to be falling down on top of me. I had been used to living near the sea and here I was in a small town in the mountains. I felt suffocated!

That first year was terrible. More than being homesick for Italy, I missed the sea. It was also strange for me to sit at the table with six people instead of 300, to eat with a knife and fork, to have a room all to myself, and not to sleep two to a bed.

I gradually adapted to my new environment. I learned French quite rapidly, and so I was able to get a job working in a home for children of unwed mothers. I worked with the four and five year olds. I had had experience working with this age group at Casa Materna. Later I went to work in a home for the aged. After that I went to work in a hospital as a nurse's assistant and here I learned how to care for sick people.

I married an Italian whom I met in the hospital where I was working. But when I met him, we were both patients there. I had just had an appendectomy and he had had a tonsillectomy. We have two children, Sara and GianFabio. Sara was married in August of 1995. She is now living in San Francisco in the U.S. because her husband's employer sent him to work there for three years. Fabio works as a mechanic in Neuchatel.

I am still living in Switzerland, but I am in close touch with Signora Livia and others at Casa Materna. I visit Casa Materna frequently and take my family with me. I developed a strong sense of responsibility toward others while at Casa Materna, and this was very useful for me in my work. After my arrival in Switzerland, I worked with children, with senior citizens, and with patients in hospitals. And after devoting myself to my family, in particular to raising my two children, I am working again, this time for the Swiss Red Cross.

Yvonne Fargnoli
Casa Materna, summer 1995
Photo: ©Fred Dole

Smashing the Odds

Francesco De Liso's Story

I was taken to Casa Materna when I was only six years old. At that time all of the children were taken there for one reason: **poverty**. It was the 1950s, the post-war period. Times were difficult for everyone. At that time our parents, especially in the southern part of Italy, had lots of children. How could they support them all? The truth was that they couldn't.

I was one of seven children, four boys and three girls. My parents were separated. They both had to work and didn't have the means to take care of all of us. Therefore, one day my father decided to distribute us among various institutions in the area. Casa Materna was the institution that I happened to end up in.

Before entering Casa Materna, I had spent all of my time in the streets. I was a scugnizzo, a typical Neapolitan street kid. The classic *scugnizzo* of the past no longer exists today. I lived in the Spanish Quarters, an area of Naples that was rundown, very very rundown. There was so much poverty. Bands of children in this area ran in the streets from morning to night. I remember that we used to have terrible fights with rocks. And I remember that, since I was one of the youngest, I always got hit. It's probably for this reason that my brain doesn't work very well today!

My father took me off the streets and took me to Casa Materna. Signora Livia, Papà Santi's daughter-in-law, says that I was terrible, really terrible. Of course I was terrible. Look where I had come from! I completed elementary school at Casa Materna but I never did finish junior high school because I was so terrible. Pastor Emanuele kicked me out because he just couldn't keep me after I had done something outrageous. What I did was truly too much.

I was kicked out because I threw a rock at one of the teachers. This teacher had slapped me in class so I ran outside, grabbed a rock, and rushed back inside and threw it at him. I missed him but I hit the wardrobe woman, an elderly German woman, who happened to be standing next to him. She had to be taken to the hospital. Pastor Emanuele immediately called my father and told him that he had to come and get me. So I went to live with my father again.

I had lived at Casa Materna for nine years. I especially remember all of the times I tried to escape from Casa Materna. I would usually escape on the train tracks that ran behind the main building. I would follow the tracks to San Giovanni where I would catch a bus to go home.

Once I disappeared for an entire week. Pastor Emanuele called my father to let him know that I had escaped. The police were probably also notified. I remember that I had to keep moving around so that no one would catch me, not even my father. Finally one day a friend of my father's saw me. He was not able to catch me by himself but had to get four other men to help him. They chased me for a kilometer and it took five of them to hold me, even though I was small. Every time I see this friend of my father's, he reminds me of this incident and says that he will never forget it.

I tried to escape because I was used to living in the streets where I had a lot of freedom. Therefore, every once in a while, I felt the need to leave because I felt so closed in. Very few kids tried to escape from Casa Materna. I was one of the few but I tried to escape often. Then when I got a little older, I was able to go outside with Signor Franceschini, the man in charge of the kitchen. I would go out with him in his car in the mornings to do the shopping. In this way I felt a little freer.

After I left Casa Materna, I didn't return to school. It wasn't like today when everyone is expected to go to school. Back then it was more difficult to get an education if you were poor.

At Casa Materna I had begun to take a course in radio technology and then I had worked a little in the carpenter's shop. I had also worked as a gardener in the vegetable garden. I had done a little bit of everything. I hadn't learned anything in particular so, when I left Casa Materna, I did a little bit of everything because that is what I had learned to do!

I began to work at odd jobs—mechanic, gas station attendant, and barman. Then for ten years I worked for Alfa Romeo. I didn't like this job very much. Finally, I had the chance to become a businessman because my father set up a little shirt factory and invited me to work with him.

Now I have my own lingerie shop in the center of Naples. I have had it now for about seven or eight years. It was difficult in the beginning but today it's going well. The location is excellent, right in the heart of Naples. I like this kind of work very much. It gives me a lot of satisfaction. I like to make deals, not big ones really but small ones. The thought of making a good deal excites me. It's like playing cards. You play to win. I sell in a rather unusual way. Maybe this is why I am able to sell so well. I buy last year's merchandise. Instead of paying 150 million lire for an order, for example, I pay 50 million lire. Then I sell it at very reasonable prices. My clients are happy. I never buy regular merchandise. With today's economic crisis, it would be very difficult to sell it.

I know that there is an economic crisis. I see colleagues who are not working. I don't feel the crisis because I have these good prices. What we all have to do is tighten our belts a little and earn less. We should not think about earning as much as we earned in past years. We must be happy with what we earn. Therefore, I try not to add much mark-up on the prices I charge; in this way I sell a lot and don't notice the crisis.

I am married and have three daughters. My oldest daughter graduated from high school and then attended the university for one year. She decided that she didn't want to continue and now works in my sister's leather goods shop in the center of Naples. My other daughters are still studying. One is studying to become a teacher, and the other, a tourist guide. I remain close to my father. I still see my mother but only rarely. She remarried and has other children. She lives very comfortably.

I live in Pozzuoli, a town near Naples. I bought a piece of land there on which I built a small villa, a little bit at a time. We are happy there because it is a beautiful house with a garden in a very peaceful area. And the school that my daughters attend is only about 50 meters from the house so that they have no problems getting to school.

Even though I was forced to leave Casa Materna, I still have very positive feelings about it. I can say that Casa Materna helped me a lot. I lived in a very bad section of Naples where there was a lot of juvenile delinquency. I am convinced that, if I had not gone to Casa Materna, I would have come to a bad end just as many of the other boys I knew did. Now I have a wonderful family, a successful business, and many good friends. Life couldn't be better! And Signora Livia and I have become very good friends.

Note: As a child at Casa Materna, Francesco may have been rather wild but he was well liked. As an adult he has the same likeable characteristics. He is open, warm, and friendly. He was one of the few children ever expelled from Casa Materna but he certainly has his life in order now and is a successful merchant in Naples. Rosaria Vincenzi calls his shop, "the most beautiful shop in Naples."

Francesco De Liso with friends
Casa Materna, summer 1962
Photo: Christine Meloni

My Best Friend Pig

Giuseppe "Lipops" Albuzzi's Story

My mother took me to Casa Materna in 1955 after my father had left her. She didn't want me to be in the middle of the street all day, Naples being what it is, you know. I was ten at the time and I cried buckets because I didn't want to leave my mother. She didn't send my brother Mario to Casa Materna at the same time. He came later.

I found it hard to make friends because I was very high strung as I still am today. For the first three months, I did not study very much so I was paired up with a studious boy whose name was Alfonso Migliaccio and he helped me a lot. He was older than I was. He facilitated my adjustment to my new life at Casa Materna. I gradually began to get used to being at Casa Materna. Everyone was very kind to me, especially Counselor Santi, Pastor Santi, and Signora Luisa. (Luisa was my brother's sponsor and later became my son's godmother.)

After I'd been at Casa Materna for about a year, Signorina Ciretta Poli arrived to take over as housemother of the younger boys. Although she was very young, she was very austere and did not put up with any nonsense. Most of us felt rather intimidated by her. Even though I had been at Casa Materna for a year, I still cried at times when I missed my mother. Signorina Poli did not tolerate crying. Whenever she would discover me crying, she would shake her finger at me in a menacing way and say, "Stop crying. You have no reason to cry. You should be happy here." Undoubtedly what she said was for my own good but I found her finger in my face very annoying. I didn't like it at all. When I reached the point that I couldn't stand it anymore, I decided to do something terrible.

One night, while everyone was sleeping soundly, I got up and ran away! I climbed up onto the wall behind the carpenter's shop and crawled along it until I was in front of the building next door to Casa Materna. Then I jumped from the wall into the street. I went on foot to Piazza Carlo Terzo in Naples, about 25-26 kilometers from Casa Materna. On foot! When I showed up at my house, my mother was shocked to see me. In the meantime, my absence at Casa Materna had been discovered, and two teachers were sent to find me. They guessed, of course, that I would be at my mother's house. They were very calm, and they gently took me back to Casa Materna. After this dramatic episode, I got used to being at Casa Materna and never tried to run away again.

I must also tell you that I soon became Signorina Poli's favorite child. Do you know why? She had an eye on a widowed uncle who used to visit me. She treated me very well indeed. She dressed me up, especially on the days that my uncle would come to visit. My uncle, however, was not interested in her because he was a very tall man, and she was too short.

Many visitors from America and England came to see us in those days. I liked being with the Americans in particular because their way of thinking was much more open than that of the Italians. They spoiled me, and, of course, I liked this. They always gave me lollipops which I adored. That's why they gave me the nickname "Li Pops" which was how I said "lollipops." These people further helped my adaptation to life at Casa Materna. I began to feel very happy there.

I was a very good student in all of my subjects (with the exception of math), and my behavior was exemplary. So I was once given an opportunity to go camping in Norway for a month. I was sent to Strandheim. When I returned to Casa Materna, I was fat, so fat that none of my clothes fit! I will never forget that experience. I have stupendous memories of it, especially the kind people, the beautiful scenery, and the delicious food.

It's true that when one is in a boarding school, one always finds a friend. I noticed a boy who was always smiling, and I like people who smile. One day I asked him, "Franco, are you happy to be here?" He answered, "Yes, I am. Of course, I like it here. We eat, we drink. Why shouldn't we be happy?" He felt that life was always smiling at him. Everything that life gave him was acceptable. Franco became my closest friend. *[Franco's—or Francesco's—story immediately precedes this one. cfm]*

Franco worked in the kitchen. I nicknamed him "Porco" [Italian for *pig*, cfm] because he would eat and eat and eat. But he always thought about me. When I went to bed at night, I would often find a piece of bread dipped in oil beside my bed. He knew what a special treat this was for me. I was always touched by his kindness.

We did so many things together. For example, we wrote comic books together. I was good at drawing the strips and he was good at writing the words. We often talked about what we would do when we grew up. Franco always said, "I will be a merchant." And in fact, he is a very successful merchant today!

Franco left Casa Materna way before I did. When he left, I suffered a lot. I cried. I was filled with anguish. I did have other friends but no one like him. He was special. After he left Casa Materna, we remained good friends. It is difficult to find true friendship. In Franco I found a true friend because, whenever I have needed someone, he has always been there for me. I have never asked him for anything but he has always sensed when I have needed something. When he needs me, you can be sure that I am always there to help him, too. It has been a real friendship that continues until this day.

I remember my last day at Casa Materna very well! In part I was very sad to leave. The Santis had an enormous party for me when I left. They also gave me a present. We all cried and kept hugging each other. In part I was happy. My mother came to get me because she and my father had gotten back together. The doctors had discovered that he had a disease of the blood and was dying. My mother wanted us to be near him in his last years. I was not only happy about going home but also because I would be able to see my friend Franco again.

At Casa Materna we were raised in an environment where we were taught to obey the Ten Commandments. I remember the stupendous sermons of Dr. Santi. And we put into practice what was written in the Bible. We were all friends and always helped each other. This is something that I have noticed among those who lived at Casa Materna. It would be wonderful if more people acted like this!

I often feel very nostalgic about Casa Materna. I am fortunate because I live close by and have the opportunity to return. When I return to Casa Materna, I feel as if time has not passed. When I look at the children there today, I see myself and my friends. In a way, I feel myself a boy again.

Without Casa Materna I would probably have stayed in my small town in Sicily, and I would never have arrived at the good position I have today. I must say with pride that I owe this all to the excellent education that I received at Casa Materna.

Note: Although Giuseppe and 'Pig' were interviewed separately, they arrived and left together. It was beautiful to see the strength of their friendship after so many years. It was also a joy to see them interact with Signora Livia and bask in the warmth of their feelings toward each other.

Resident children with volunteers David Mason (Scotland),
Michelle Squadrini (U.S.), and Pastor Bob Bronkema (U.S.)
Casa Materna, summer 1996
Photo: Casa Materna Archives

The Choice: Italian Military Service or Switzerland?

Giacomo Noto's Story

I was born in a small village in Sicily where everyone struggled very hard to survive. It was right after World War II. I remember that my father worked when he could. The daily necessities were scarce. But in spite of this situation we were a very happy family and satisfied with the little that we had.

Unfortunately our happiness did not last long. Our mother became ill and died. In her final months her children were her major preoccupation. She realized that our father couldn't take care of us on his own so she discussed this problem with the pastor of the Protestant church in our village, He promised to be responsible for us. After her death he contacted the Santis, and they kindly agreed to take us in. I know that Casa Materna saved me from a life of abject poverty and made it possible for me to achieve a secure and respected position in society.

I remember the day I arrived at Casa Materna as if it were today. We left Sicily on October 3, 1956. Our father accompanied us. To pay for the trip he had to ask for help from his relatives. When we arrived at Casa Materna, we were greeted by Fabio Santi. He was very affectionate with us but this was not enough to overcome the great trauma of saying goodbye to our father. I remember the desperate cries of my brother (he was barely five at the time). Our father had to leave us without saying good bye in order to avoid the pain of the separation. Thus began our first day at Casa Materna.

My brother and I gradually began to make friends and to enjoy being with other children and the trauma of the separation began to fade into the distance. I remember the days full of activity. The regular school day was very demanding and was followed by lessons of singing and of music. Then, when we became older, vocational courses were added for the boys such as carpentry and mechanics.

I was especially tied to four friends at Casa Materna: Francesco De Liso [see Francesco's story above. cfm], Guido Cosentino, Vittorio Bianchi, and Emilio De Cesare [Emilio is currently an employee of Casa Materna. cfm]. I remember Francesco's generosity. His father came to see him every Sunday because he lived in Naples and he would always bring something for his son. Francesco would then always share it with me because my father was too far away to visit me.

I left Casa Materna when I had reached the age of almost 18 and received an ugly surprise: a letter from the military calling me to service. Pastor Emanuele said to me, "You have two possibilities:

leave immediately for your military service or, thanks to some acquaintances in Switzerland, we can find you a job there." Naturally I did not have to think twice about this offer. My choice was Switzerland where I am still living today.

I was very emotional on my last day. I was about to begin my life as an adult. Pastor Emanuele in his final speech at a small going-away ceremony for me told me to honor the reputation of Casa Materna by living the way I had been taught. He accompanied me to the station and told me to return whenever I wanted to. In fact, he gave me the money for a return trip. I almost bought that return ticket immediately upon my arrival in Switzerland!

I arrived in Switzerland in February 1965, and I began work. At the beginning I found life in a foreign country where I didn't know the language very difficult, and I felt homesick for the places I had left behind. But I began to to attend a local church with services in Italian. The pastor was a very dear person. Here I met my wife. We have a daughter who has grown up too fast and will soon graduate from high school!

I used to see Pastor Emanuele often because he would come to Switzerland for conferences and concerts to raise money for Casa Materna. With the passing of the years, I have become completely integrated into this nation. After 27 years I consider it, without a doubt, my second country.

Giacomo Noto with his wife
Casa Materna, summer 1995
Photo: ©Fred Dole

An Enchanted Life

Bianca Avagliano's Story

My parents had seven children but they were very poor and couldn't take care of all of us. They heard about Casa Materna through a Protestant minister living in Salerno and decided to send their three oldest children there. I was the oldest and I went to Casa Materna along with my sister Anna Maria and my brother Silvio. The four youngest children remained at home.

I lived at Casa Materna for nine happy years. The Santis were like our parents. Perhaps they were even better than our own parents because they really did love us and did many things for us. My relationship with my own father was not very good. I don't know very much about him, and I don't want to know anything. But I love my mother who was, and still is, very attached to all of her children.

When I was at Casa Materna, my parents did not come to visit me every Sunday as many other parents did. They would come every 15-20 days or so. This made me very unhappy, and I used to cry on the many Sundays when they did not come. But they always came to get me for the holidays, and I was very happy then although the holidays always passed quickly.

Casa Materna used to have two special schools for the girls, an embroidery school and a sewing school. I took lessons in embroidery. I loved to embroider, and I became very skillful at it. In fact, whenever the teacher was unable to come to school, I took her place and taught the other girls. This experience was a wonderful one for me, and I am still enjoying the fruits of this experience today. I am now a professional embroiderer. I have many clients. I make things for brides—very beautiful trousseaus—lingerie, blouses and other clothes, curtains, tablecloths, everything. For ten years I taught embroidery to girls in my home.

In Italy, especially in the South, we are very tied to our families, to our traditions. My husband is a fine person. He has given me a happy life, a beautiful house, three children. We are a very united and happy family. Our oldest daughter Giovanna has a diploma in bookkeeping and is about to finish her degree in law. She plans to become a judge. She is married and has one child. Our other daughter Cinzia also has a diploma in bookkeeping and is studying law at the university. My son is still a student as well.

I go back to Casa Materna almost every year for the anniversary celebrations in June. I take my children with me. They always remark that Casa Materna is "an enchanted place, a marvelous place." It *is* an enchanted place, and I feel such nostalgia when I think about it. You know, my umbilical cord is still attached to Portici, to Casa Materna. Sometimes when I argue with my husband, I say, "I am leaving, I am going back to Casa Materna." And he says, "Go ahead. Then I won't have to feed you anymore!"

Note: Bianca Avagliano radiates happiness. She came to the interview eager to share her fond memories of Casa Materna and to show off her two beautiful daughters. All three were wearing lovely blouses that Bianca herself had embroidered.

Law and Order

Luigi Civitella's Story

I was born in Naples but I have always lived in Portici. I am Neapolitan. My parents, too, were Neapolitans. Do you find that hard to believe because of my red hair? Haven't you ever seen a Neapolitan with red hair? My father had red hair, too. It happens! Here in Portici everyone knows me and knows that I am Neapolitan. But when I leave Naples and find myself in other places in Italy, people rarely take me for a Neapolitan. They usually think that I am a foreigner, not an Italian. When I say that I am from Naples, they say, "It's not true!"

I entered Casa Materna in 1956 at the age of 5. My mother had died of an incurable disease, and my father couldn't take care of four children ranging in age from three to six. Two of us were put in the care of the Santi family and the other two were taken to another home in Portici called Pennese.

I used to stay at Casa Materna all summer. Few of the children went home for the summer. We were fortunate to have our own beach at CM. The water was almost always clean. Every once in a while one of the ships dumped oil deposits (tar) in the water. But it was usually clean. Now it is polluted, not with tar but with the wastes from the factories.

I remember that when I was at Casa Materna there was a religious service every morning before school at 9 o'clock. Every evening we gathered together to say grace before dinner—everyone, adults and children. Every Thursday we sang in the chapel before dinner. We took turns singing—first the older children, then the younger ones. Then one of the children recited a Psalm that he/she had memorized.

My worst memory of Casa Materna was my brother's death. It happened on December 12th, 1962. When classes let out at 4 pm that day, my brother Renato ran to the stairs and began to slide down the bannister. He fell off the bannister into the stairwell from the second floor. He died on the way to the hospital.

I left Casa Materna in 1969 because I had to leave for my military service in the Navy. And it was time for me to choose a path for my life based on the education and experience that I had received during my years at Casa Materna.

After finishing my military service, I signed up to become a policeman. I decided to become a cop because I was very attracted to this profession. I did my initial training in Bolzano. In Italy police forces are not local as in the States but national. They are housed in the Ministry of Internal Affairs. There are several police academies, and new recruits are sent for training wherever there is an opening. That's why I was sent from Naples to Bolzano. After my training, I was sent all over half of Italy—Milan, Brescia, Florence, and Rome—before finally returning to Naples.

Times were different when I became a cop. Now the risks and dangers have increased. Naples is one of the most dangerous cities, especially the area around Herculaneum, because it is the land of the Camorra. The Camorra makes life difficult for us here in Naples. Every three or four weeks someone gets shot. There are massacres.

Many criminals are caught and sent to prison but do they *stay* in prison? That's the question. The answer is, "No." Many foreigners think that the Camorra is the same as the Mafia. That's not true. In Sicily there is the Mafia. In Naples there is the Camorra. They are two different organizations.

I have traveled all over Italy but I prefer Portici to any other place. I live in the heart of Portici, right in Piazza San Ciro. I go to Casa Materna often, and I am always heartily welcomed. It is a place of peace where one feels far from the city. There is a strong sense of peace, of freedom. It is so full of green, so far from the outside world. But you take one step outside and you find yourself again in the midst of chaos. Casa Materna itself never changes; it is only the children who change.

I am pleased to maintain my contact. Casa Materna has influenced my life a lot. If I had not been able to come to Casa Materna, I would most likely have been abandoned to the streets because my father had to work and could not look after me. My life there was a fabulous experience. We were all family and there were no distinctions among us. We learned to respect others and to help the weak. The words that come into mind when I think about Casa Materna are those inscribed on the main building: "Let the children come unto me." This is the most beautiful sentence of my life.

Boys playing in the nursery
Casa Materna, summer 1995
Photo: Casa Materna

From Resident Child to Casa Director

Rosaria Russo's Story

I entered Casa Materna at the age of ten. I remember my great amazement at the beauty of Casa Materna's gardens and how I felt a tremendous sense of peace. I also remember being surprised at seeing so many children together in one place, especially in the dining hall where, despite the high number of children, there was very little noise.

I remember one person in particular who impressed me with his kind, serene nature and that was Papà Santi. He was a man who enkindled in me feelings of great affection and great respect. He was the father and the grandfather that I had longed for but had never had.

I remember Signora Livia, Papà Santi's daughter-in-law, who, despite her young age, was able to guide so many girls of different ages and to give each one of us a sense of duty, of respect, and a desire to improve ourselves and to work hard to obtain what we wanted. I studied hard because I knew that only in this way would I be able to tear myself away from the moral and material poverty that was all around me.

I had an American sponsor while I was at Casa Materna, Janet Hubbard from California. She has been like a second mother to me. She attended my wedding and has been present at all of the other important events in my life. She still writes to me every week, and I am very grateful for all of the interest and love that she has shown to me throughout the years.

My sister Silvana's sponsor, Mrs. Marjorie Hendricks, offered me a great opportunity. She invited me to go to the U.S. to study business for one year, first in Washington, DC and then in Bridgeport, Connecticut.

The last day that I spent as a resident at Casa Materna was truly rich with excitement. I was leaving with a group of American friends who were returning to the US after a visit to Italy. I can still remember Pastor Emanuele's words of farewell: "Rosaria, may God be with you during this coming year and remember that we at Casa Materna will always wait for you because Casa Materna is your home. And remember that you will have a secretarial job waiting for you here." I remember that these words greatly encouraged and stimulated me. I wanted to show these people whom I loved so much that their hopes and expectations were not in vain.

I can certainly say that my stay in the United States was the most important event in my life and the beginning of new hope and new horizons. I received a diploma that I would not have been able to earn in Italy at that time because such studies were very costly. My studies in the U.S. were, of course, also expensive but the very generous Mrs. Hendricks paid for them for me. It's wonderful to be able to tell the whole world that, even though, on one hand, my life was deficient in many things, on the other it was and is rich in satisfactions, blessings, and human contact.

I had less difficulty adjusting to life in the U.S. than I had in adjusting to life in Italy upon my return. I returned to an Italian society that was then completely different from American society and I, therefore, had to make a great effort to keep the freedom of thought and of action that I had gained in America.

When I returned, I received job offers from several international companies because of my knowledge of Italian and English and my excellent secretarial skills in both languages. But I had another commitment. Pastor Emanuele and the whole family at Casa Materna were expecting me, and after a few days I began to work in the English Correspondence Office.

A few years after returning from the States, I married Pietro who had also grown up at Casa Materna. We have two sons, Nico who has a degree in law from the University of Naples, and Andrea who has a degree in communication. Both sons are great gifts from God, and I consider myself very very fortunate.

I served as the Director of Casa Materna for several years. It is clear that Casa Materna will always play an important role in my life. Casa Materna has certainly influenced my life in a very positive and marvelous way.

Rosaria and her husband Pietro Vincenzi
Casa Materna, May 1993
Photo: Christine Meloni

Living the American Dream

Silvana Russo's Story

I was only three when I entered Casa Materna. I was not told very much about why I was taken there but I learned later on that my mother had been left alone with seven children after my father had abandoned her. She was unable to take care of all of us so she took three of us (the youngest) to Casa Materna.

What I really liked about Casa Materna was that I was always surrounded by many friends. We developed friendships that were strong and close because we were all in the same boat. There was a very strong feeling among us to help each other, and these feelings kept us going.

Today, whenever my teenage daughter complains that she doesn't have enough clothes, I remind her of my experience at Casa Materna. Each girl had only one outfit, and we had to share underwear! Every Saturday night we took off our clothes and gave them to the laundry ladies. We then took our weekly shower before going to bed. On Sunday morning we were each given a set of clean underwear which we would wear until the following Saturday.

I had an American sponsor, Mrs. Marjorie Hendricks. She was the owner of the Watergate Inn, a restaurant in Washington, D.C. She was very generous and kind. I remember receiving lots of goodies from her for Christmas and other holidays including my birthday. She even came to visit me at Casa Materna. I certainly remember her as one of the brightest aspects of my life at Casa Materna.

The Americans did a lot for Casa Materna. The English and the Dutch did, too, but it was the Americans who were more visible. I remember the trips we took to visit the American ships stationed in the Bay of Naples. These outings offered us one of the few opportunities we had to leave the confines of Casa Materna. And also they gave us the chance to spend time with Americans who, in our minds, represented the hope of a better future. We saw handsome young Americans on these beautiful ships. They prepared special lunches for us that were delicious, and they gave us many presents.

I became close friends with an American volunteer at Casa Materna, Betsy Guinn. After she returned to the States, she wrote to invite me to spend a year at her home in Linden, Massachusetts. Just before my departure, I met a very kind American man who had come to Casa Materna to visit a boy that he and his wife sponsored. He invited me to spend my first Thanksgiving with his family in Schnectady, New York.

When I met his wife, I immediately loved her. She was a second-generation Italian. She struck me as the perfect mother, kind and loving. I also fell in love with their 20-year old son Mark who was a college student at the time. In March of the following year we became engaged, and in September we were married. My decision to stay in America was very easy at that time because I was in love. And it wasn't difficult for me to adapt to life in the U.S. When one is young, everything seems possible.

We now live outside of Philadelphia. I have adapted well to life in America, and I am very happy here. However, the older I get, the more time I want to spend in Italy. I feel the need to experience the same things that I experienced before I left. I also feel the need to teach my children about Italian life, to make them understand where their mother comes from. And I have remained a Neapolitan at heart.

I should say that Casa Materna has influenced everything that I am today. Living at Casa Materna I learned one very important lesson and that is that every action that we take affects others. Therefore, I learned to respect and live with others. When you share everything with one hundred other girls, you develop skills that are essential to live harmoniously with others. I cannot say what would have happened if I had not gone to Casa Materna. I was the youngest child and never grasped the reality of my family situation. We are all born with a certain something that stays with us all of our lives, and I believe that I would have been a fighter, but having been steered in the right direction, all that fighting was put to good use.

Casa Materna gave me lots of other skills: how to take care of the house, embroider, sing, dance, and act. And I learned to have an appreciation for the real beauty of life. It wasn't always easy living without the love of parents, but I realize now in my wise old age that in the long run I am a better person for having lived at Casa Materna.

Silvana Russo
Casa Materna, Christmas 1969
Photo: Casa Materna Archives

Homesick in Minnesota

Nunzia Calore's Story

My mother did not have a husband but she had several daughters. When I was only two years old, she decided to take me to Casa Materna because she was not able to take care of me. I cried a lot in the first few years because I missed her. I would sit next to a wall on the second-floor terrace outside of the girls' living quarters and cry. I almost caused that poor wall to disintegrate with my tears! I would sit there, crying and waiting, especially on Sundays, parents' visiting day. I would wait and wait for my mother but she never came.

Then, when I was six years old, something happened that caused my whole attitude to change. It was during the Christmas holidays. Most of my friends were getting ready to go home, but I was not able to go. One day Pastor Emanuele called for me, and I ran down the stairs as fast as I could. I was hoping with all my heart that I would find my mother waiting for me. But I was greatly disappointed. Instead of my mother, I discovered one of my aunts.

The Pastor said, "This woman is your aunt, and she wants to take you to your mother's house. But I told her that it was not possible because I want you to stay here with me. I have good reasons for my decision. Now go back upstairs." I shouted, "But I want to go home to my mother!" I went upstairs and cried. After a while the Pastor called me back and we had the following conversation:

Pastor Emanuele:	Your real parents are those who feed you, who clothe you, who are near you when you are sick. So—who feeds you?
Me:	You do, Pastor.
Pastor Emanuele:	Who clothes you?
Me:	You do, Pastor.
Pastor Emanuele:	Who sends you to school?
Me:	You do, Pastor.

From that day on I did not miss my mother anymore, and I never cried again.

I was ten years old when I met Mr. And Mrs. Tom Anderson from Minnesota during one of their visits to Casa Materna. They liked me very much. In fact, they even asked if they could adopt me. The Pastor said that it was not possible because the court had not yet officially consigned me to Casa Materna. The Andersons decided, therefore, to wait for three years until I had finished junior high school. They then asked me to stay with them for one year. If I was happy there, I could stay for good; if not, I could return to Casa Materna. Their hope was, of course, that I would stay with them. The Pastor told me that, if I stayed, I would be able to study and I would have a better life.

Before leaving for America, the Pastor asked my mother to come to Casa Materna to say good-bye to me. I had not seen her for eight years. I felt strange, really strange. I wanted to go near her but, at the same time, I didn't want to. Even though she was my mother, she was a stranger. It was at this meeting that my feelings for her were completely extinguished.

It was a long way from Portici to Biwabik, Minnesota. I had to go to Rome to get a flight to Boston. In Boston I was supposed to catch a flight for Minneapolis but I missed it because I had fallen asleep at the airport. I was not at all used to life outside of Casa Materna. I had always lived at Casa Materna and had gone outside only on very rare occasions. The following morning the flight attendants took me by the hand and accompanied me onto the plane bound for Minneapolis. In Minneapolis I caught a flight for Duluth. The Andersons met me at the airport there, and we then drove to Biwabik which was a four—hour drive from Duluth.

I had two major problems when I arrived in the U.S. The first one was the way of life. Since I was used to the strict discipline at Casa Materna, it was a shock to find myself all of a sudden with so much liberty. To live so alone so suddenly! I felt like a small puppy left on his own to face the world. I didn't know anything about socializing in the outside world. The American kids were so free. They left their homes, they went to movies, they organized parties in different locations. I was unable to adapt to this kind of social life. I preferred to stay at home by myself. The Andersons encouraged me to go out but I didn't want to. Actually I liked staying at home because the house was so beautiful. It was like entering paradise. I had never had a room that was all mine, a bathroom that was all mine, a closet all mine, a mirror all mine. I liked staying in this special environment that the Andersons had provided for me.

The second problem was the language. The Andersons did not speak Italian. They had to use a bilingual dictionary a lot. The first day I was there, they invited a girl named Teresa to their house. The daughter of Italian immigrants, she could understand Italian although she could not speak it very well. She was able to translate for me. However, on the second day, the Andersons said that I would have to begin to learn English. It was not difficult for me to learn English. After a month I was able to understand English well. I didn't speak it too well but I could make myself understood. It was the way of life, however, that remained difficult for me.

I immediately started going to school. Everything was strange for me. I got along all right, however, even though it was really a different world. The school was very beautiful and much better organized than the schools in Italy. I had attended a junior high school in Portici near Casa Materna that was really horrendous. The building was dirty and in a state of disrepair. The classrooms were cold. The desks were very large, and many children were squeezed into one desk. Rarely did we have physical education.

At first everyone stared at me in school because I was a novelty for them. I felt intimidated. Gradually, however, I began to make friends. Every morning I had two classes of English, one with the 9th graders and the other with the 10th graders. I also had two hours of art. I loved this class because I liked to draw very much. I could have stayed in the art class all morning! In the afternoon I had another hour of English which was a speech class. I also had classes in business typing, physical education, and home economics. In this last class I made my first dress.

I stayed in Minnesota for 18 months. Then I decided to return to Italy. I was very homesick, especially for Casa Materna and also for my boy friend. When I had gone to the States, I had had to leave the boy that I had just met on the beach of Casa Materna. (At that time Casa Materna had a beautiful beach. People from all over Portici went to our beach.)

I was simply not able to adjust to the life in America. I had become accustomed to a very disciplined life at Casa Materna. There was a strict schedule that never changed. At a certain hour there was Bible study. At a certain hour there was the daily worship service. Meals were served at certain hours. And one had to adapt to the wishes of the majority.

The Andersons were naturally very disappointed. They didn't want me to leave. In fact, they bought a round trip ticket for me hoping that I would return to Minnesota within a short time. They told me, "You can go back to Italy now; but in case you want to come back here to us, you have a return ticket which is good for six months." But, after returning to Casa Materna, I couldn't leave again. I was attached to the place where I had grown up. I felt immediately at home. I adapted right away to my old way of life.

When I decided to leave Minnesota, not only the Andersons were disheartened but also Pastor Emanuele was very disappointed. He told me that I had thrown away a wonderful opportunity. The Andersons would have let me finish high school, and they would also have sent me to school to become a flight attendant. (They had also promised me a piece of land as a dowry.)

Even though it had been my dream to finish high school, the Pastor did not let me continue my studies in Portici. He said that I had to begin looking after myself, to face life by myself, and to accept a little responsibility. I had lost forever my chance to study.

After I returned from the States, I discovered that my mother was ill. I tried to help her as much as possible. This was another reason that I did not go back to Minnesota. While she was sick, I was always there next to her. She said that she didn't deserve my concern and assistance. I told her not to worry about that. I tried to help her as much as I could until she died. I stayed with her until the very end.

Before she died, my mother said, "I took you to Casa Materna so that they could take care of you, so that you could have a better future. If you ever need anything, go there and ask them for help. Go there even if you need work." In fact, I did go to Casa Materna and I was given a job. I feel that my mother's wish has come true.

I am still working at Casa Materna. Now I work with the younger boys. When I returned from the States, I was only sixteen years old; therefore, I could not work with the younger boys then because they lived in the same building as the older boys. Instead I began to work with the girls. For me it was like returning to Casa Materna as a child. I lived with the girls, and I had to live as they lived. For example, I had to get up when they got up and I had to eat breakfast with them. Then, every morning at 9 o'clock, after the girls had gone to school, I went to the office to work with Rosaria. She was supposed to train me to work in the office, but I soon discovered that I was not cut out for that kind of work.

When I turned eighteen, I got married. The wedding was held in the chapel at Casa Materna. Dr. Teofilo was the one who gave me away. After the wedding we had a beautiful party under the portico of the main building. Shortly thereafter we experienced difficulties because my husband lost his job. But Signora Livia gave him a job as a blacksmith in the workshop at Casa Materna. We have two sons, Luigi and Massimiliano. I try to maintain a strict schedule with them so that they will grow up to be decent and well educated individuals.

I did not sever my ties with the Andersons. I am still very attached to them, and I am always in touch with them. In fact, two years ago I went to visit them along with my husband and children. They are very attached to me, and they write to me often. If all goes well, they will soon be coming to Italy to visit me.

But I am glad I returned to Italy and Casa Materna. I have so many beautiful memories of Casa Materna that I cannot give my affection to any other place, to any other people. Children are bound to their surroundings. Casa Materna is my home; it is where my roots are. I cannot survive away from Casa Materna. When I am far away, I am like a fish out of water.

Dr. Teofilo always said, "Yes, a flower needs to be planted but it also needs to be cultivated." It's not enough to plant the seed. A plant needs to be cared for day after day so that it will grow, so that it will bloom. Casa Materna cultivated me—continues to cultivate me—and I will always be grateful.

Note: Nunzia has blonde hair and fair skin. She could easily be taken for a Scandinavian or an American from Minnesota. In fact, she says that in Italy people often think that she is an American.

Nunzia Calore with older boys
Casa Materna, summer 1995
Photo: ©Fred Dole

A Love for Math

Salvatore De Martino's Story

I think that I found myself at Casa Materna principally because there were so many of us at home and the financial resources were very sparse. So my parents decided to put two of their nine children in a home. Their choice fell on me and my brother Egidio who was two years older than I. They chose Casa Materna because my father was a Protestant and felt that it would be the best place to give me the kind of education that he wanted me to have. Also my parents knew that the directors of Casa Materna were highly respected.

I don't remember my first day too well but I remember that it was summer. When I was taken to Casa Materna, I was taken down to the beach on the Gulf of Naples that belonged to the Home. This made me lose my feeling of homesickness, and I adapted readily to my new life without any psychological problems.

I remember also that I found at the Home another school friend who lived in my section of town whose name was Fabio Vitiello. We became best friends and continued to see each other even after leaving Casa Materna. I will always remember my friends, the directors, the sense of humanity that they always had for us and today I can say also the great spirit that they had to keep such an enormous structure on its feet, even sacrificing themselves physically.

I appreciated very much the work activities that were carried out inside Casa Materna even though I must say in good conscience that I was never a great worker. I remember fondly the instructor of carpentry. I also remember the great soccer challenges held in the square between the school and the railroad tracks. We all chose our favorite teams and, since I wanted to be the strongest, I chose Juventus, the team that always won everything.

I also remember the school teachers but especially the math teacher who succeeded in making me love math so much that I considered it my favorite subject and even today I benefit from this love. How can I forget how pleasant it was there where there were also girls and this made us feel less isolated from the outside world. I experienced my first crushes at Casa Materna! My first crush was on a girl named Lucia Petrella. There were happy moments in which we exchanged glances stolen when the others were not looking.

These are memories that fill our imaginations and I talk about them as if it were yesterday.

CHAPTER 6

Common Memories

Certain themes recurred in the residents' narratives. To avoid frequent repetition, some of these common memories are gathered together in this chapter. First names are used except when that name is shared by other individuals.

The Santi Family

That the members of the Santi family were greatly loved comes out clearly in the narratives.

Yvonne: When I think about Casa Materna, I think about how lucky we were to be with the Santis who were such refined and well-educated people. They loved us even though we were not their children, and they taught us the values of life. They gave us healthy bodies and healthy spirits.

Papà Santi

Luigi di Somma: In my mind's eye I can still see a heavenly figure in a white robe arriving at 5 every afternoon to conduct the service. We jokingly called this figure, our dear Papà Santi, "The Ice Cream Man!"

Giuseppe Zampino: Papà Santi loved all children. Whenever he saw a child in need, he did not hesitate a minute before welcoming him/her to Casa Materna. He was short, very short, but he was very active, very energetic, always in motion. He never stopped. He was the one who took care of the discipline of the children. He was the one who found the food for the children. He took care of everything! I remember that when I got a nail in the bottom of my shoe one day, he was the one who personally medicated my foot.

Mamma Santi

Luigi di Somma: I will always remember an important lesson that I learned from Mamma Santi. One Sunday, before the church service began, she asked us if we had money to put in the offering plate. None of us had anything to give. Smiling she then lovingly gave each one of us a few coins. At the same time she advised us to save some of our money so that we too could make contributions. "*Listen, my dear children. There are many people who give money for you and for our church. Therefore, you too must collaborate by making small offerings so that people can see that you children too serve as good examples.*" These kind and dear words stimulated many of us to save our money in order to make offerings on Sundays and not to waste our money on useless things.

Luigi di Somma: I remember with much sadness and pain the death of dear Mamma Santi, due to an illness. The loss of that holy woman was really tremendous for all of us at Casa Materna because she was a woman who knew how to give joy, love, and affection to anyone. Between her and Papà Santi there was a true competition of goodness! We were all very fond of her, and we knew that with her we lost a piece of the history of Casa Materna.

Giuseppe Zampino: Signora Ersilia Santi was a person with a noble spirit, a very altruistic woman. She loved children very much and was very sensitive to their problems.

Emanuele Santi

Franco: Every once in a while we were taken to concerts. It was usually Pastor Emanuele who was responsible for organizing these outings because he wanted to impart his love of music to the children. He and I both played the violin. Every morning we were the first ones to begin practicing, me in the school building and

Pastor Emanuele in his study. Often he listened to me, and he would later tell me about my mistakes in playing the high notes.

Bianca: One of my fondest memories is the time I broke my leg while playing with my friends one day in the garden. I was happy about it because, whenever it was time for meals, Pastor Emanuele would say to me, "Bianca, climb onto my back." I would climb onto the tall man's back and he would walk very carefully down the many stairs to the dining hall. Perched high in the air I would immediately become the center of everyone's attention. What a happy memory!

Bianca: I remember that whenever we needed anything, like a pair of socks, we would go to Pastor Emanuele. We would say, "We need 500 lire or 1000 lire." He would ask, "What do you need the money for?" We would say, "We need to buy some socks." And he would give us the money. He was just like a father. He was wonderful. Of course, we would also buy ourselves some candy along with the socks!

Bianca: And how could anyone forget Pastor Emanuele playing his violin! He would wake up early and play his violin. Every morning I was awakened by violin music. What a beautiful way to wake up!

Giacomo: I think of Pastor Santi often. Every time I hear or read the verses of the 23rd Psalm, I think of him and Casa Materna. It was Pastor Emanuele's favorite psalm, and he referred to it often in his sermons.

Fabio Santi

Luigi di Somma: I also remember well that, when it was summer time, Fabio Santi would organize wonderful trips to magnificent places, but I remember that I was particularly happy when we took trips to Capri. It is one of the most beautiful islands in the world. We went there in a large motor boat, and, once we were there, we swam and we ate in the countryside in the meadows in bloom. We played and had lots of fun. Then before leaving, we would sing hymns and pray to the Lord, thanking Him for the great joy of the magnificent day we had spent together.

Luigi di Somma: Within a short time after Mamma Santi's death, grief hit Casa Materna again: the sudden and unexpected death of Fabio Santi who died in an automobile accident on his way to Rome. This loss too overwhelmed Casa Materna because Fabio Santi was the animator and the organizer of everything. In addition to his position as director, he also was responsible for keeping close ties with both our Italian and foreign supporters. From him came every positive initiative for Casa Materna. Therefore, his death was very upsetting and disruptive.

Teofilo Santi

Luigi di Somma: Like his parents, Dr. Teofilo was an excellent man in every way. He was the doctor who took care of us when we were sick. He also offered his medical services free of charge to those living in the vicinity who could not afford to pay. It is difficult to forget these valiant men of faith who truly loved their neighbors as Christ has taught us to do. Dr. Teofilo dedicated his life to Casa Materna and had kind words for whoever worked for the good of others. He taught all of us what it really meant to be good Christians. When he saw me doing things that I shouldn't do, he would scold me in a paternal way and make me reflect. In this way he taught me that in life the more one reasons and reflects the fewer mistakes he makes.

I remember with great happiness the day that Dr. Teofilo married Signora Livia. That day was truly blessed by God. That marriage brought happiness and joy to Casa Materna. And I remember that Dr. Teofilo wanted all of the children to be present at the celebration because he considered us all his little brothers and sisters and wanted his joy to be our joy as well.

Franco: Just before his death Fabio had promised to buy a television set for us older boys. But his brother Dr. Teofilo kept Fabio's promise for him. Actually we received one of the first television sets in all of Italy. Our TV was the first one at Casa Materna. Not even the Santi family had a television yet. Sometimes Dr. Teofilo would stay with us a while to watch it.

Nunzia: I remember one year at Easter time Dr. Teofilo took us to Mt. Faito. When we arrived there, he said: "Here is a hill. Run up it as fast as you can. The first one to the top will win a prize." Everyone began to run up the hill, shouting excitedly as they ran. I decided not to participate in the race. Instead I walked over to Dr. Teofilo. I took his hand and I squeezed it. And he said to me, "Very good. You have done something beautiful. I see that you need this hand to guide you." He was so struck by my action that he continued to remind me of it right up until the month before he died.

Signora Livia

Rosaria: I remember Signora Livia (as we called her) who, despite her young age, was able to guide so many girls of different ages and to give each one of us a sense of duty, of respect, and a desire to improve ourselves and to work hard to obtain what we wanted.

Rosaria: I remember that each one of us had a score card, and we were given points when we succeeded in accomplishing something. When we reached certain goals, we were given marvelous prizes. This taught me to be proud of myself and gave me the desire to improve myself always and to leave behind me my past and the thousand difficulties that I had experienced.

Special Days

The Annual Anniversary Celebration

Every year in June, on the Sunday closest to Papà Santi's birthday, the children put on a spectacular show of music and dance for Casa Materna's anniversary.

Giovanni: There were many beautiful moments, especially the holidays and the anniversaries. For Casa Materna's anniversary each year we prepared a very well-organized program with skits, songs, and gymnastic performances. I was always one of the protagonists because I had acting ability and a decent singing voice. The director of the program was Fabio Santi who was then a student of Agrarian Studies at the University of Naples.

Luigi di Somma: Among my many happy memories I remember the celebrations for Casa Materna's anniversary every June. All of us, from the youngest child to the oldest, awaited these magnificent celebrations with great eagerness. And we all worked hard to make them a great success. It is difficult to describe this special day. One needs to be there to realize what it's like. If one thinks about a fair that has everything, that is what it's like. The anniversary of Casa Materna is an indescribable joy for everyone. It is *our* celebration. It is very important just like Christmas.

I remember that these festivities were always very well organized by the Santi family and the staff. All of the children worked hard to prepare for it. The choir practiced a lot and was always wildly successful. There was a lot of competition among the children because our relatives would be coming as well as many foreigners.

The program was very vast. All of the children, residents and non-residents alike, were involved. Several months ahead of time we began preparing the plays to dramatize, the songs to sing, and the acrobatics to perform. The choir practiced Neapolitan songs and ancient Italian songs. Our band prepared pieces from operas, from foreign national anthems, and other important musical pieces. There was really a festive air in the days of preparation. We did everything that we could to prepare well because we knew that it was a very important day for Casa Materna. Many people would come to watch our plays, to hear us sing, to listen to the 30-piece band, and watch the acrobatics.

The audience was always pleased with the performances and applauded greatly. The foreigners took many photographs to take back to their countries to witness to that great work of God that was called Casa Materna.

Antonietta: I remember the anniversary celebrations that took place every June. We spent months preparing for these celebrations. We prepared dances. A real stage was set up outdoors for our dances! I remember that one year the workmen put up an absolutely

enormous stage! I think it was for the 50th anniversary of Casa
Materna. I remember that that day was magnificent. And the
grounds were full! There were so many people! I remember all of
the special days because they were different. On those days we
laughed a lot and we did crazy things.

Christmas

Giorgio: I remember the huge Christmas trees covered with
lights and many beautiful things and the plays we prepared for
Christmas.

Luigi Di Somma: I can never forget the celebration of the
Christmas tree. This was another occasion that filled our hearts
with joy. We prepared for it with plays and songs related to the
events of the birth of Christ. And I remember especially that, in
addition to preparing for a magnificent celebration for a very large
audience, the older boys worked in the carpentry shop making
wooden toys that we put under the Christmas tree along with
other gifts. After the performance every child received gifts. That
which tickled us the most was that many of us received gifts that
we had made with our own hands!

Giacomo: I have wonderful memories of Christmas. It was a
much-anticipated festivity because, in addition to the plays and
the songs that we prepared for the very numerous spectators, there
were always presents for us under the very beautiful Christmas
tree.

Luigi Corti: Back then Christmas was very special. Our
preparations were exceptional. We made beautiful things to put
under the Christmas tree, we performed plays, our famous choir
sang, and our wonderful band played. I loved the music. Whenever
I hear hymns on TV now, I always think about Casa Materna.

Antonietta: I remember Christmas time very well. We used to
perform plays in the auditorium. Then we would receive the gifts
that Signora Livia had prepared for us. This was wonderful. In
fact, I continue this tradition with the children who come to study
at my house. I give each one of them a small gift for Christmas just

as I always received gifts as a child at Casa Materna. I really feel like doing this. Something inside me urges me to do it. Even though I don't have a lot of money, I always give each child a small gift.

Silvana: I remember that at Christmas time we would be invited to a private club in Naples by the wives of Americans who worked for NATO in Naples. These women invited us for lunch and then they gave us candy, which was something that we rarely saw at Casa Materna. Sweet memories!

Easter

Franco: In Italy the day after Easter is called "Little Easter" or "The Monday of the Angel," and it is a national holiday. On this day officials from the NATO would come to Casa Materna and hide chocolate Easter eggs on the grounds for the children to find.

Antonietta: At Easter time we received chocolate eggs or other things. Again I carry on this tradition with my children and with my students. There is a voice within me that says, "You must do it." This is something that I always do. It reminds me of my childhood and it makes me feel happy.

The Strong American Connection

Food Assistance

Franco: I remember that American ships arrived in the port of Naples with bags of flour, containers of butter and cheese. Casa Materna became the distribution center. Under the school building there was a huge garage (big enough for two school busses). All of these goods were kept there. The lights of the garage were kept on continuously and there was a guard on duty there.

I was around 14 at the time. Along with the other older boys I would help unload the big trucks when they arrived at the gates of Casa Materna. We would carry the cans of cheese and other small things. There were workmen to carry the heavier things. A large part of this food stayed at Casa Materna for the children.

Therefore, I can say that I was at Casa Materna when there was an abundance of food.

The rest of the food was distributed to other Protestant churches, especially those in the South. The distribution went as far as Sicily. When I was a child, I would go to Sicily to visit my grandfather who was a leader in the Waldesian Church in Messina. When the supplies would arrive, the flour, the cheese, the butter from Casa Materna, we would go around to deliver them to the people who needed food whether they were from the Church or not.

Luigi Corti: There was an abundance of food in the years I was there. Frequently, trucks would arrive at Casa Materna full of American food. There were large quantities of cheese. We ate a lot of cheese, really a lot! These trucks also brought cans of other American food. I especially remember a kind of chocolate cake; it came in a can but it was still very delicious.

Visits of U.S. Military to Casa Materna

Franco: When I was at Casa Materna, American sailors used to come to visit us often. There was one I knew in particular who knew that I collected stamps and he always brought me some.

Giuseppe Albuzzi: When I was at Casa Materna, the Americans would bring us small tins of beef. For some strange reason I wanted to save mine so I would make a hole in the dirt and hide them. Do you know that one day, many years after I had left Casa Materna, I went back for a visit and decided to see if the tins were still there. I started digging and I found my old tins! There they were, after all of those years! Of course, there was mold in the tins! We boys always had our secrets. It is wonderful remembering this particular secret of mine.

Visits To American Ships

Franco: We visited American ships docked in the port of Naples. Sometimes they were battleships but usually they were aircraft carriers. The sailors would give us tours of the ship. They would show us these huge elevators that carried the airplanes from one level to another. And we watched the planes take off just a few meters away from us! Before lunch the sailors would show us Walt Disney movies in the original English. Sometimes they would put on a show for us. Then we ate and the food was always in great abundance. Before we left we were always given presents—toys, balls, dolls, games. I think that we visited almost all of the great aircraft carriers many times—the Saratoga, the Forrestal, the Intrepid, all of the ships of the Sixth Fleet.

Giacomo: The visits that we had the opportunity to make to the American military ships were wonderful and very interesting. To see ships big enough to have airplanes on them personally excited me very much. These visits served as recreation for me but also to awaken in me a passion for airplanes which led me to my current position with an airline company.

Antonietta: I remember our visits to the American aircraft carriers in the port of Naples. When we arrived, the sailors would give us a tour of the ship. They would give us rides in the huge elevators that were used to move the airplanes from one level of the ship to another. I was really impressed. These elevators were huge! I remember riding up in one of these elevators. When we arrived at the top, there was the sky! It was a magnificent scene. Absolutely beautiful! What wonderful memories!

Each sailor was assigned one child. I remember once my sailor actually took me inside one of the airplanes and pretended to fly it! After the tour we would go downstairs to eat lunch and then we'd watch cartoons. We didn't have cartoons yet in Italy so this was a real treat for us. Then before we left, we were given gifts. The sailors gave us chocolates, chewing gum, little packages. We all returned to Casa Materna with packages in our hands. I will always remember the kindness of these people. I remember during one of these visits a sailor gave me a little pin—I still have it today! I was nine or ten at the time. In my life I have moved around a lot, and I have lost many things. But I have never lost this pin! I keep it as a good-luck charm. I have had it now for more than forty years!

Silvana: I loved the trips we took to visit the American ships.

They offered us one of the few opportunities we had to leave the confines of Casa Materna. And also they gave us the chance to spend time with Americans who, in our minds, represented the hope of a better future. We saw handsome young Americans on these beautiful ships. They prepared special lunches for us that were delicious, and they gave us many presents.

Giuseppe Albuzzi: I remember that when we were good we were rewarded with trips to the aircraft carriers. We would always receive surprise packages from the sailors. After lunch onboard ship, the sailors would give us these gigantic packages with many many wonderful things inside—candies, chocolates, and clothes.

U.S. Navy Sailor with Daniela Santi circa 1960
Photo: Casa Materna Archives

Casa Materna children on board U.S. Navy ship circa 1960
Photo: Casa Materna Archives

Visits To Homes Of Americans In Naples

Franco: I remember that I always stayed at Casa Materna during the Christmas holidays. A lot of the children did. Some of us were invited by officers of the NATO to their homes for dinner. Not everyone was invited to these special dinners. Only about 30 or 40 of us would be chosen to go, those that had worked the hardest and deserved a reward. We would eat in different homes and then we would all meet in one of the homes for something special. I remember one year a magician put on a show for us. I remember that in one of the houses that I visited the host had an electric train that took up half a room. I watched it work for over an hour!

Antonietta: I remember that I was once invited to stay with one of the American NATO families for a week during the Christmas holidays. I went with my friend Felicetta. We felt as if we were in America! When we returned, we told everyone that we had been to America!

Sponsors

Luigi di Somma: My sponsor [in Italian *padrino,* cfm*],* if I remember correctly, was from New Jersey. He wrote to me often, and I was happy that someone across the ocean thought about me. But I must tell you that I was disappointed with him many times because, every time he wrote to me, he sent me a newspaper written in English. Unfortunately I couldn't read it because I didn't know English. I was also disappointed because, while the other boys received toys and special gifts from their sponsors, I always received this English newspaper which, to tell you the truth, I didn't appreciate very much! Every once in a while he would send me $10 but always this newspaper that I couldn't read! I would like to have changed sponsors. In his letters (which were translated for me) he always talked about his beautiful house and about his family. He often talked about Italy because he had done his military service in Italy during the war. He always talked about returning to Italy and coming to visit me. Although he never did, he has remained one of the many memories of my youth spent at Casa Materna.

Giuseppe Zampino: I had a sponsor, Mr. Newton Bell, in California whom I met during our U.S. tour. We were scheduled to perform in California but he couldn't wait for me to arrive there so he came to meet me in Colorado Springs! It was a very emotional meeting. After the concert ended that night at 11 p.m., we got into his car and drove to California. I spent two marvelous days with him in Los Angeles. He was a very wonderful and affectionate person. He had learned about Casa Materna from Pastor Emanuele who was the ambassador for Casa Materna in the United States. He helped me with my studies. He never came to Italy and unfortunately we were not able to keep in touch after I left Casa Materna.

Ciro: I had a sponsor from Holland whose name was Dirk Leonard Broeder. He was a teacher who lived in a small village called Nebilt near Utrecht. Mr. Broeder was one of the many Dutch friends of Casa Materna. He became interested in Casa Materna when he saw a film prepared by Dr. Teofilo that aired on TV in Holland. As you know, until very recently Casa Materna received virtually no help from within Italy; therefore, there was a lot of activity designed to make Casa Materna known in other places in the world. He was a real father to me. Every year he came to visit me in Italy and would take me camping. After I left Casa Materna, I went to his home in Holland many times. My first visit was in 1960. I like the Dutch people very much. They are very warm and friendly. My generous sponsor died in 1989 but I am still in touch with members of his family who are scattered around Holland. We take turns visiting each other. I was just there to visit his family at Easter time this year.

Bianca: Every child had a sponsor. We wrote to our sponsor every month and our sponsors sent us gifts. I had two sponsors, a man and a woman from the States. Unfortunately I've lost touch with them. They sent me many wonderful things like chocolates, chewing gum, clothes, dolls, puppets, things that children like. We were always so happy when packages arrived from our sponsors. When they arrived, we were called to the office to get them. We were always on our best behavior when we went to the office! We would open our packages and then write a thank-you note. When I think about these days, I feel so nostalgic.

Antonietta: We always received packages with gifts from our sponsors. These packages were always full of wonderful things. When I was at Casa Materna, every child had a sponsor. There were, therefore, lots of sponsors, in particular people from NATO.

Luigi Corti: We all had a sponsor. Mine was an American who sent me gifts. Twice a month I would receive toys from him. I remember in particular that he sent me a marvelous Kodak camera. He also sent me money.

Rosaria: I had two sponsors while I was at Casa Materna: Mr. and Mrs. Harry Spoon and Ms. Janet Hubbard. I stayed in close touch with the Spoons, and we saw each other a couple of times. Mr. Spoon died several years ago but his wife is still living, and we continue to write to each other often. Ms. Hubbard has been like a second mother to me. She has followed me all of these years. I am very grateful for all of the interest and love that she has shown to me throughout the years. *(See Appendix A for Janet Hubbard's account of her sponsor experience. cfm)*

Silvana: I had two sponsors, Mrs. Hendricks and Ms. Janet Hubbard. Mrs. Hendricks was my sponsor when I was little. She was the owner of a restaurant in Washington, D.C., the Watergate Inn. She was very generous and kind.

Janet Hubbard was actually my sister Rosaria's sponsor. When she came to Casa Materna for a visit, however, when I was eleven, she took me under her wing and became my godmother as well (and also a little bit Renata's). She remains to this day one of the most important people in my life. I still keep in close touch with her. Even though she lives in California, we talk to each often on the phone and we manage to see each other at least once a year. She is like a mother to me, and now she is the grandmother of my children. This wonderful woman has taught me by example that the most important things in life are love and kindness. She is "Mom Janet" to me; I love her like a mother.

The Boys' Band

Music played a very important role in the life of the children at Casa Materna, especially in the years when Emanuele, a very talented violinist, was the director. All of the children participated in the choir while only the boys became members of the band.

Giuseppe Albuzzi: My friend Franco was envious of me because I was more musically inclined. I could play the horn, but he couldn't play any instrument except the cymbals. But he really couldn't even play them; he always played at the wrong time. One day we were practicing "Aida." Maestro De Gregorio was on the platform with his stick, and Franco played out of turn in the grand finale.

"Animal!" Maestro De Gregorio shouted. As he yelled, his stick slipped out of his hand and hit me right in the face. Franco began to laugh. "There!" shouted Maestro De Gregorio. "If I had known, I would never have let you take part in the fanfare!"

Although Franco had no musical talent, I did and music became a very important part of my life at Casa Materna. I played in the band and I also sang in the chorus. I will always remember the wonderful joint concerts of the bands of Casa Materna and the USS Forrestal that were held in our beautiful gardens near the fish pond.

Giorgio: I still remember that I studied music and played the trumpet in the small band that, accompanied by Fabio, was invited to play on national holidays at places outside of Casa Materna. I remember the arrivals of Emanuele from the United States with his magical violin.

Giovanni: At the age of ten I joined the fanfare as a trumpeter. I was in the first row of the fanfare, not because I was the best, however, but because I was the shortest!

Giuseppe Abbellito: We had a band, and we enjoyed playing in it. We played for the pure pleasure of it. I learned to play the trumpet. We also enjoyed participating in the choir of Professor Dragoner from the Conservatory of Zagreb. Professor Dragoner was a political refugee.

Luigi Di Somma: There was a professor of music, Maestro Alfredo Bonavolontá, who taught those of us who wanted to learn to play instruments. We had a band that played on certain important occasions or when we had visits from foreigners and so it was important that the children learned to play. In my last years at Casa Materna I played the drum in the band because I did not have much musical talent and I didn't want to learn.

Salvatore: Another likeable person was the music instructor, Professor De Gregorio. Music was the activity that I enjoyed the most, even though the instrument that they taught me was not, at the time, the one I preferred. However, I had the satisfaction of becoming one of the first to play the clarinet and for this I will always thank those that gave me the opportunity to do so and today I am very sorry that I did not continue my studies of music. These are mistakes that we pay for in life and today I am trying not to make the same mistake with my children and in fact I am having my older son take guitar lessons.

CHAPTER 7

Celebrating the 90th Anniversary: June 1995

The First Alumni Reunion

Every year in June Casa Materna celebrates the anniversary of its founding. Some of the alumni living in the Portici area attend. But there had never been an official alumni reunion. Rosaria Vincenzi and others decided to track down as many alumni as possible and invite them to return to Casa Materna for the 90th anniversary. The reunion was very well planned by a committee chaired by Cristiano Capuano, Papà Santi's great grandson. Almost 100 former residents returned to relive their childhood memories. Many supporters of the Home were also present to celebrate the landmark occasion. People came from the Naples area and other cities in Italy as well as Germany, Holland, Switzerland, England, the United States, and Australia.

The week-end festivities were kicked off by an outdoor concert on Friday evening. Many residents of Portici attended this event along with the children and guests of the Home.

On Saturday morning the elementary school children and teachers did not go to their classrooms as usual. Instead they gathered outside in front of the main building to practice their dances for Sunday's anniversary program one last time. From any spot on the grounds of Casa Materna the music and laughter could be heard as the children danced and sang. The air was electric with excitement. After many weeks of enthusiastic preparation, the moment of the children's eagerly anticipated anniversary performance had almost arrived.

As in many past years the rehearsal was supervised by the dedicated and experienced Signora Livia. While she was the loving mother looking over her fifty children, she was also the sharp-eyed critic, desiring and demanding perfection from her children. The annual anniversary celebrations are always an enormous success, not only because of the children's charm but also because of their nearly flawless execution. The anniversary is one of the highlights of the year for them, and the enormous pride they have in the program is clearly visible.

Saturday afternoon was warm and sunny. The children were free to play. Some of the housemothers for the boys bought small plastic swimming pools, and delighted shrieks rang out as the boys jumped in and out of the water. They managed to get a hold of the hose, and adult visitors not keen on getting drenched stayed as far away from the boys as possible.

All of the children then had a picnic dinner in the garden so that the dining room could be prepared for the gala alumni dinner.

Throughout the day excited alumni continued to arrive and the dinner was attended by approximately 70 alumni, most of them with their spouses and some with their children as well, and guests from many countries. This special dinner was held in the dining room where all but the two oldest alumni had eaten so many meals as children. Giovanni Stoecklin and Giorgio Quinzi, both now in their 70s, had lived at Casa Materna when it was located in Via Cimbri. They attended with their spouses. [Their individual stories can be found in Chapter 3.]

Some of the alumni met childhood friends that they had not seen for more than 20, 30, in some cases 40 years. These encounters were powerfully moving. One notable meeting was between Antonietta Romano and Yvonne Fargnoli. These women had been close friends while growing up and had left Casa Materna on the same day in 1963 to go to Switzerland. Yvonne had remained there but Antonietta had returned to Italy in 1965. [For their individual stories, see Chapter 5.]

Many adult men were moved to tears at the arrival of their former housemother Signorina Poli, now 80 years old but still very much in command of her faculties. Much to everyone's amazement, she recognized all of her former boys and many of the girls as well. And she had many tales to tell!

Miss Poli played a crucial role in the lives of hundreds of children who had lived at Casa Materna. She had ruled the dormitory of the younger boys (ages 6-11) with an iron hand for 35 years. She instilled terror in the boys who feared her more than they loved her. But seeing her again after many years, they came to the realization that she had set them on the right path and deserved their lasting gratitude and affection.

No other housemother had come close to staying as long as Miss Poli. Several of the girls at the dinner boasted about how adept they had been in getting rid of their housemothers, and they mocked the boys for not being able to dislodge Miss Poli.

As has been the habit at Casa Materna since its founding, the following grace was said before the meal began:

> Padre Santo, Padre Buono,
> Questo cibo e' il tuo dono.
> Dallo anche ai poverelli,
> Perche' siamo tutti fratelli.

English Translation:

> Holy Father, Good Father,
> This food is your gift.
> Give it also to the poor,
> Because we are all brothers.

The seven-course meal began with prosciutto and mozzarella followed by baked macaroni, roast beef and peas, sausage, mixed salad, and strawberries with lemon. The attendees, however, were so busy greeting each other and reminiscing that they had little time to pay much attention to the delicious food that was placed before them, the best food that Casa Materna had ever seen. Italians love to eat, southern Italians in particular, but at this special dinner, much of the food remained untouched, even plates of pasta!

Everyone did pay attention to the final course, the special anniversary cake and champagne. The cake which was divided into two parts, one in the shape of a nine and the other a zero, arrived in the midst of great fanfare. Glasses were filled with sweet Asti Spumante, and everyone present was in the mood to drink to Casa Materna's 90 years.

After the conclusion of the dinner many strolled through the grounds of the villa enjoying the fresh night air or wandered to the terrace facing the Bay to breathe in the familiar smell of the sea water and to catch a glimpse of the lights of Naples in the distance. No one wanted the magical evening to end, but there was more to look forward to on the following day.

Sunday morning heavy rains pounded the Italian peninsula from north to south, east to west. Miraculously, however, a gorgeous sunny day dawned in the Naples area. The many fervent prayers of Casa Materna's friends had indeed been answered. (A rumor quickly circulated that many individuals would have become atheists if rain had spoiled the Anniversary festivities.)

The Methodist Church of Portici was full on Sunday morning. The service in this church on the grounds of Casa Materna was one of the main highlights of the week-end for many. Alumni sat in the pews where they had sat every Thursday evening and every Sunday morning as children. Few eyes were dry. The service was movingly conducted by the two pastors from the United States, Bob and Stacy Bronkema. A children's choir sang several hymns. There was a full bouquet of ninety red roses on the altar, one for each year of Casa Materna's existence.

The most moving moment of the service was Giuseppe Sfameli's introduction of Nicodemo Smerglio, a 94-year man who could very well be the oldest living former resident of Casa Materna. He lives with relatives in Vasto near Portici. When told by his relatives that he could not attend the anniversary because he was too old, he sneaked out of the house and caught a bus to come to Casa Materna. Needless to say, he was greatly admired for his spunk and determination and greeted excitedly by many of those present. He was driven home after the service and was then picked up and brought back for the children's performance in the afternoon.

During the afternoon the main pathway of Casa Materna was bustling with activity. Booths had been set up to sell food and other items such as ceramic pieces, embroidered goods, stationery; all proceeds were destined for Casa Materna. Residents of Portici joined alumni and guests for the anniversary festivities.

The long-awaited performance of the children began promptly at 5 o'clock. The program was as follows:

Children's Program

Kindergarten—A March
Fourth grade—The Joy of Living in Peace
Fifth grade—Hula Hoop
Second grade—The Gypsies
First grade—When the Cherries Are Ripe
Kindergarten—The Traffic Light: Policemen in Skirts
Third grade—Dutch Dance
Second grade—Playing on the Beach
Fifth grade—Mexican Dance
Kindergarten—Musical Chairs

After the children's program, there was a break followed by a series of performances by local singing groups. The music lasted until around 11 p.m. Few alumni and guests were willing to call it a day, and animated conversations and joyous laughter were heard way into the wee hours of the morning.

The reunion was declared a triumph, and everyone agreed that it should become a tradition. The comments that the alumni wrote in a journal book passed around by Rosaria reflect the impact this event had. Below is a small sampling of entries.

Journal Entries

"It has been a great pleasure for me to return to Casa Materna, a mythical and unforgettable place. Words are superfluous because there are no words to describe what I would define as a fairy tale. I thank Casa Materna for everything that it did for me and thousands of other children. I hope that it may continue its good works for needy children. Thank you from my heart."

—Paolo Petrarolo

"It has been an immense joy to see so many friends again. Such emotions! May God continue to bless the efforts of everyone."

—Yvonne Polizzi Faragnoli

"I thank God that He placed you of Casa Materna on my path, you that were always near me, assisting the steps of an uncertain child. I love you and I will always save a special place for you in my heart. I love you all. You are great, Casa Materna!"

—Domenica Mercogliano

"I am immensely happy to be here to remember the happy times and to live again in the maternal womb. This home is, and will remain, for me a maternal womb from which it is difficult to cut the umbilical cord. To say "thanks" is too little. There are not words to express how much gratitude I feel for this home. I hope to remain forever in your hearts as you are in mine. With affection."

—Silvana Spina, The Sicilian

"On this day I have rediscovered myself."

—Roberto (from Caserta)

"This anniversary has been the most beautiful encounter of my life."

—Giacomo Noto

"For one day I have felt the same as I did 40 years ago."

—Valentino Costabile

Children's Anniversary Essay Contest

An essay contest was held in occasion of the 90th anniversary of Casa Materna. The children currently attending the elementary school were asked to write essays on the theme "What I Like Best about Casa Materna." The winning essays from each grade can be found in Appendix C.

CHAPTER 8

What You Can Do For Casa Materna

An Appeal from Massimo Finoia

Naples is a city that is famous throughout the world for the beauty of its panorama, its sea, and its sun, for its songs as well as its pizza and its spaghetti.

But it is also famous for its *scugnizzi*, the Neapolitan street urchins known for their flair and their liveliness, true protagonists of the popular life. But the stories of the *scugnizzi* are not always happy stories. The hunger and the poverty in Naples, as in all large cities, often slowly entice the *scugnizzi* on the path of contraband, of minor theft, of purse snatching, leading them in the end to commit more serious crimes.

How many *scugnizzi* has Casa Materna snatched from this destiny in its almost one hundred years of history, during which it has taken in, educated and put on the straight path, thousands of children? Certainly many hundreds.

This fact alone sheds light on the importance of Casa Materna and its good works and the need to see that it has the financial resources to continue its work. Its work is even more necessary today in a society in which the drug traffic has induced many young people into the world of delinquency. And, in addition to the *scugnizzi* of yesteryear, there are many young people who have emigrated from Third World countries who need food and an education that will permit them to take their place in their new country with dignity.

What you can do:
Some suggestions from Rosaria Vincenzi

1. Pray for the children, their families, the staff, and the benefactors of Casa Materna.
2. Sponsor a child. You can be an individual sponsor. You can form a church, civic, or professional group. Or you can organize a small group of your friends.
3. Organize a fundraiser, e.g. a spaghetti dinner or a musical evening.
4. Collect school supplies, clothing, sheets, toys, and games for the children.
5. Form groups to go to Casa Materna for a short work project, e.g. a week of painting or two weeks of gardening.
6. Make a donation to the U.S. Casa Materna Society, Inc. Donations sent to the U.S. organization are tax deductible; donations sent directly to Italy are not.

APPENDIX A

Sponsor Narratives

Over the years many individuals have volunteered to sponsor children at Casa Materna. Below are two narratives written by American sponsors whose lives were marvelously changed by their experience.

My Italian Daughters
Janet Hubbard's Story

Little did I know when I received that first picture and letter from a young Italian girl at Casa Materna that we would share such an affectionate relationship and many happy experiences together. Or that after my first trip to Italy for Rosaria's twenty-first birthday, I would become Mom Janet to three Italian daughters.

This all happened thirty-five years ago when I sponsored a child through the Christian Children's Society. The Society was affiliated with Casa Materna and the lovely child was Rosaria Russo, now Rosaria Vincenzi.

After four years of correspondence, I met Rosaria in 1964. She was living in Connecticut and attending a business college. After many letters and telephone calls, I arranged for us to vacation together in Connecticut and to attend the World's Fair in New York City. Our relationship as mother and daughter developed during this vacation and has remained very close ever since.

In 1969 I flew to Italy for Rosaria's twenty-first birthday, also meeting her younger sisters Silvana and Renata for the first time. Rosaria was working at Casa Materna and all three girls were living there. By the time I returned to California, I was Mom Janet to three daughters. It was during this visit, when Rosaria and I spent part of the vacation at Casa Materna, that I met Pastor Emanuele Santi. He was a very compassionate man who worked tirelessly for the children. Our friendship continued during his many speaking tours in California and my visits to Italy.

In 1971 Silvana came to New York to live and attend school. We strengthened our mother and daughter relationship on vacations together in California and New York before her decision to marry and live in the United States. She was the first of the three girls to marry. The wedding was a joyous occasion when the four of us had one of our numerous reunions in New York and when I met Silvana's husband Mark McKinlay.

There have been many other trips over the years to spend vacations together. Two special occasions that we celebrated in Italy were the christening of Nico, Rosaria's and Pietro's first son and my first grandchild, and the wedding of Renata to Peppe Barreca.

Rosaria and Pietro have two sons. The four of them have spent vacations with me in California. Silvana and Mark have two children. Since they live in the United States, we have been very fortunate to spend time together each year.

This past December 1995, we had a wonderful reunion at Silvana's and Mark's home outside Philadelphia where they now live. Rosaria and Nico arrived from Italy and I flew in from the West Coast. This was a very happy time for all of us.

All three daughters are very caring, thoughtful people. Now we continue to share the loving relationships that started so many years ago with my sponsorship of a child from Casa Materna.

Long Beach, California
1995

Our Neapolitan Daughter-in-Law
Al and Ann McKinlay's Story

We began to feel the need to help poor children in 1963. That was the year we took in our first welfare boy, little David aged 14 months whom we kept for five months until he was adopted. About the same time we also decided to do something for children overseas and thought Italy would be the place since that is where Ann's parents came from. We signed up with the Christian Children's Fund and were assigned little Domenico from Casa Materna.

We sponsored several children from Casa Materna between 1963 and 1970. That was also the period in which we took in our last two welfare children and eventually adopted Steve and Jon, now 30 and 29 years old, respectively. Then Al had a business trip to Milan in May of 1970 and tacked on a side-trip to Portici. There he met Pastor Santi and also Rosaria Russo (Vincenzi) who introduced him to most of Casa Materna's kids including her little sister Silvana. He was amazed at the beauty of Casa Materna amidst the squalor of Portici.

Shortly after his visit Al decided to deal directly with Casa Materna as a sponsor with firsthand knowledge of the place. In October of the same year both of us made a trip to Europe and included a stop at Casa where Ann was introduced to Rosaria, Silvana, and the other kids. We also met Betsy Guinn of Boston who was working there at the time.

In the summer of 1971 we heard that Silvana was coming to the U.S. to complete a final year of high school as a guest of the Guinns. Since we had been favorably impressed by both girls, we decided to invite them over for a weekend in the fall of 1971. We noticed right away that Silvana was a very natural, outgoing, happy, and helpful person who participated in everything even though her English was a bit rough. One would never have guessed that she had spent most of her life in a children's home.

Well, one weekend stay led to another as Silvana and Betsy visited many times during that school year. In the beginning, our 21-year old son Mark had a sweetheart and did not pay too much attention to the girls. But that all changed one June day in 1972. Mark asked his mother, "How can I get Silvana to go for a ride on my motorcycle without leaving Betsy out?" Ann replied, "Why not have your riding buddy Dave come up and then suggest that all four of you go for a ride? Then hand your extra helmet to Silvana as you get ready to leave with Betsy taking Dave's." It worked like a charm.

From then on the two were inseparable. Silvana came over almost every weekend and when she didn't, Mark cycled 200 miles to Boston. When she went home for the summer, he couldn't stand it so he flew to Naples by himself and looked around until he found her. They became "steadies" for all of Mark's senior year at college, getting engaged in March and talking about marriage after he graduated from college in June of 1973.

Naturally we were quite pleased at the turn of events. This would be the first of our kids to be married. Also this gave Al an excuse to plan a really grand event, something he does often in his work of conducting large conferences but not something ever done for a personal event. In addition to planning for the wedding, we also entertained Rosaria and sister Renata as guests for a month prior to the wedding. On a sad note Ann's mother died rather unexpectedly two weeks prior to the wedding.

September 2, 1973 dawned very warm and became even warmer as the day wore on, hitting 95 degrees while the reception and dancing were going full blast. Everyone had a terrific time (especially Al). We sent the newlyweds off in the family car for their honeymoon in Niagara Falls. They were back in two days, however, because Silvana's passport wasn't accepted at the Canadian border due to her new marital status.

For most of the first twenty years of their marriage, Sil and Mark lived within 25 miles of our home, and, as a result, we saw them almost every week-end. From 1985-1993 they lived only a mile away, and we saw them and their kids almost daily. Our whole family is a closely-knit one, and we work at keeping it that way. There is no question that the family is the fabric of society and when it tears, much of the good in it will fall out.

Silvana became a second daughter even before she married Mark, and nothing has changed that feeling. We often disagree, mostly about the Italian vs. American ways of doing things, but never to the point of long-lasting ill will. She is as sincere a person as one could ever hope to find. We consider her a true member of the McKinlay clan, a great addition to an already disparate group, yet adding to the synergy that is the real meaning of "family."

Pattersonville, New York

Silvana, Rosaria, and Luke
Lake near Philadelphia, October 2002
Photo: Mark McKinlay

APPENDIX B

The Children's Choir: The Pride of Casa Materna

The American pastor Joel Warner organized the children's choir and led it on the triumphal Grand Tour of the United States in 1956. This tour was an unforgettable experience for the economically-disadvantaged children of Casa Materna. Joel tells about his involvement with Casa Materna, in particular with the choir, and about the Swiss and U.S. tours.

Pastor Joel Warner's Story

The Warner family first connected with Casa Materna through my mother (who was not yet a "Warner") when she met Luisa and Mamma Santi in the 20s and traveled with them to Naples. She lived there for a long time and was always a close part of the Santi family. My mother and grandmother, then, sponsored Emanuele when he came to this country and my parents found a home for Luisa and Franz and three of their five girls when they moved to the States in the late 40s.

I went to Casa Materna, at my mother's suggestion, following graduation from college in 1953. I had intended to work for a year, but I ended up in a committed and full time relationship with Casa Materna from October of 1953 through August of 1957. During the time I was there I started the English correspondence office together with another American volunteer, Miss Lena Ware. I wanted to do something with the children but didn't know what. Since I have a musical background, I decided that we would start a choir as an activity that the children could participate in during the long evenings. Although I didn't realize it at the time, putting teenage boys and girls together in such an activity in Italy was a bit risqué, but the results in terms of music were so good that the Santis let me get away with it.

I also had younger children in the choir. We sang a cappella mostly because I could not play the piano and no one else could, either. We began to sing in the church at Casa Materna and then in the Methodist Church in Naples. Then we sang at the cornerstone laying of the new evangelical hospital that Teofilo had built.

From there emerged the dream to go on tour among our Protestant churches in Switzerland—and we did! I can still remember that great experience: 24 or so kids, Fabio, myself and our bus driver in the great conservatory hall of music in Geneva where we received a standing ovation. The other memorable experience was singing at the tomb of Giuseppe Verdi in the courtyard of the old folks home that he had endowed in Milan. There we sang the song that we all loved to sing the most: "Va Pensiero" from Verdi's Nabucco. I can still remember the residents of that home putting their heads out the windows as we sang. So many memories! As I write this, I am remembering Giuseppe Zampino. He was full of the devil during that trip and we had to keep a special eye on him!

Then, of course, when we returned to Casa Materna at the end of October 1953 (bringing a large supply of Swiss chocolate for the kids who had not made the trip) the dream to come to America was born. I returned to the States in January of 1955 with the goal of organizing that tour. I did so from the parsonage of Emanuele in White Plains, New York, where he was pastoring at the time. I continued to work and plan, returning to Casa Materna in the summer of 1955 for a few weeks. The children, with Fabio and a much more expert director, came to the U.S. in January of 1956 and we toured from New York to California, from Minnesota to Texas until July of that year before returning to Italy. It was during our time on tour that the sad news came that Mamma Santi had died. There was much sadness on the part of us all, especially Fabio who was very close to his mother.

From July of 1956 through August of 1957 I continued to work at Casa Materna: English correspondence, host to visitors, directing the choir again. Fabio was tragically killed during the last week of October of 1956. By then I had already planned to marry Ida Masri who had grown up at Casa Materna and return to Yale Divinity School. The plan worked out with Fabio was that after graduation I would return with Ida to serve with him as a co-director. That, of course, never materialized because of his untimely death. However, in April of 1957, Ida and I were married: a civil service in Portici, a great reception at Casa Materna, and then another religious service in Ida's hometown of Faeto. Emanuele was the officiating minister.

I worked very hard for Casa Materna from 1957 through the mid-1970s. Together with Ida and two of my three children I returned to visit in 1962 and again in 1972. When I returned in 1972, part of the mandate I had from the church I was serving then was to find a child whom we could sponsor and bring to the States for a year. That young man was Aldo Vincenzi, the brother-in-law of Rosaria.

My son spent a summer between his junior and senior year in college at Casa Materna. As a result, he was inspired to become a teacher with elementary school children. I myself am a minister today because of Casa Materna, in general, and because of the great inspiration of my mentor, Fabio, and Papà Santi. One of my proudest moments as I remember it now was returning in 1972 to preach a sermon in Italian. How I wish that Papà Santi could have been there to hear it! Actually his spirit was in that beloved chapel, I am sure.

New Jersey

APPENDIX C

What I Like Best about Casa Materna:

Essays by Children

Here are the winning essays from the 90th Anniversary Essay Contest. It is very clear that what the children appreciate the most about Casa Materna is the natural beauty of its setting. It is an oasis in the midst of poverty.

EMANUELA (first prize winner, second grade)

As soon as I come through the main gate of Casa Materna, I say to myself, "How beautiful this park is!" There is a round fishpond and there are even fish inside it. Then there are the white benches to sit on. The playground has a slide, a little merry-go-round with wooden horses, and swings. There are fragrant flowers in the gardens, a little woods with a house for squirrels, and many growing plants. It is a splendid garden. From the window of my classroom I can see the blue sea, the sea-gulls that land on the water, and the sky that is always blue. In the spring I can see the swallows that fly into the sky. I come to Casa Materna to learn how to study.

ELOA' (second prize winner, second grade)

The first time that I saw Casa Materna I was struck by the very big green and flowering garden in front of the school. The children were all outside waiting for the teachers and I was excited about being there with them. My eyes kept looking at the trees, the paths, and the pond with many fish. At Casa Materna there is also a playground with games but what I like the best is the very big and very beautiful green garden with its flowers and the large space in which to play and have fun.

VINCENZO (first prize winner, third grade)

In my opinion, Casa Materna is very beautiful! The gardens that surround it, the view that one can admire from the windows, the persons that live in it, everything impresses me. I especially like the view that I can admire when the sun is shining; at this time Casa Materna is even more beautiful. The gardens are very special because of the palm trees surrounded by very beautiful flowers, the beauty of the pines, and the beauty of the statues hidden among the flowers.

When I enter Casa Materna, I feel like I am in another world because I can admire the view on one side and the beauty of the immense garden on the other.

Here in this beautiful place I am able not only to admire nature but also to study and learn many things. It is lucky that Casa Materna is here because there are many things to do in this immense villa, even for those who are no longer children.

ANGELO (first prize winner, fourth grade)

I have been at Casa Materna for four years. Casa Materna has a very beautiful central lane that is full of trees and aromatic flowers and also blackbirds, robins, and sparrows. It also has an infirmary because, when we play, we might get hurt. At the end of the main lane there is a fountain full of water and many fish. In the middle of the fountain there is a white statue of a man with a vase on his neck.

Casa Materna has a very big garden full of trees. Around it there is a lot of space for parking cars or for playing. In the school building there is the office of the director. What I like best about Casa Materna is that the main lane is surrounded by many flowerbeds full of scented flowers and trees. When spring comes, it is wonderful to look at this lane because it resembles a beautiful painting.

MICHELA (first prize winner, fifth grade)

I have been at Casa Materna for five years and for me it is like my second home. I am happy here because there are many children for me to play with.

Casa Materna is very big and very beautiful and there are several beautiful places that I like. I like the huge garden with many flowers and many trees and the big fishpond with its little red fish.

It is very romantic in the afternoon when I go to a place that is very special to me and watch the sun set. It is also very beautiful before school in the morning when the pastor holds a service. I like it because it is nice to dedicate a little of our time to Jesus.

There is a wide lane full of palm trees and, while one walks along it, one can see in the distance the sea that breaks its waves upon the rocks. When we are in the dining hall, it is nice because all of the classes are together and there is a joyful atmosphere.

At Casa Materna there are many trees and for this reason we breathe pure air. There is no problem with polluted air. Casa Materna is beautiful and often tourists come to visit my school. I like my school very much, and I am very happy that I come here to school. I will never forget this school because I have passed the happiest moments of my life here.

Children of Casa Materna
Casa Materna, circa 1990
Photo: Casa Materna Archives

CASA MATERNA
BIBLIOGRAPHY

Davey, C. (1982). *Casa Materna: The Santi story.* Casa Materna Society, Inc.: Tuckahoe, New York. [Copies available from the U.S. Casa Materna Society.]

Goetz, H. Jr. *The Casa Materna story coloring/activity book.* [Copies of this multilingual coloring book for children may be purchased from the Casa Materna Society Office Administrator.]

Meloni, C. F. (2000, Summer.) Casa Materna: An orphanage in Naples offers children a future. *Ambassador: National Italian American Foundation Quarterly,* vol. 45. [Copies of this article about Casa Materna and about Franco Maccarrone are available from the National Italian American Foundation.]

Meloni, C. F. (2001, Fall.) Tale of two sisters from Naples, Italy. *Wells Express.* [This article about Rosaria and Silvana Russo appeared in the alumnae magazine of Wells College, Aurora, New York.]

Porret, E. (1978.) *Enfants de Naples: La merveilleuse histoire de Casa Materna.* Cachot Press: Switzerland.

Relevant Addresses

American Casa Materna Society
Office Administrator, Mrs. Evelyn Taggart
639 Westchester Road
Colchester, CT 06415-2224
Tel./Fax: 860-267-4096

Casa Materna Society, Inc.
P.O. Box 176
Tuckahoe, New York 10707

National Italian American Foundation
1860 19th Street N.W.
Washington, D.C. 20009
Tel. 202-387-0600
Fax 202-387-0800